GOOD TO GROW

'Steve Tibbert's intentional leadership in building a diverse and culturally relevant church that is not just good but great is more than obvious, it's contagious. I consider it a privilege to have experienced Steve's leadership and mission-focused community at King's. I fully commend his work to you as biblical and practical.'

Dr David Anderson – Senior Pastor of Bridgeway Community Church, Cleveland, USA and author of Gracism

'Any church leader who wants his church to grow will benefit from reading this book. Steve writes with honesty and insight about the remarkable growth that he has experienced at King's Church, Catford. The result is a powerful tonic to mediocre leadership. Anyone who reads this book will finish it challenged and equipped to lead more effectively and with greater wisdom than ever before.'

David Stroud – Senior Pastor, ChristChurch London and Leader, Newfrontiers family of churches in the UK

'You hold in your hands a book that recounts a captivating story of how our great God has been working through what was once a small church in south-east London. When a visiting prophetic team spoke of a vision from the church's history that had been lost, little did they know that a student of C.H. Spurgeon had begun this congregation with a dream of building a 1,000-member church. Just a few years later, King's Church is now one of relatively few British churches that regularly gather more than that number. Some books on church growth erroneously tell you that if you just follow a set of principles you will automatically experience the same results. Others equally wrongly speak only of a sovereign work of God. This book is different. You will see evidence of the grace of God, but you will also learn from both the mistakes and successes of the church's leadership team. Rick Warren says that any church that is content to stay small is telling the world that they don't care if they go to hell. God may not be calling your church to be as large as King's, but he is calling you to faithfully learn from others and apply leadership lessons, and work hard to make disciples of all nations. You may not agree with every aspect of the philosophy of ministry you will find in this book, but reading it will definitely help you better understand the way in which God is calling you to serve in his church.'

Adrian Warnock – blogger and author of
Raised with Christ

'This is a book for leaders who really want to work with God to grow their church. It's practical and realistic. And it doesn't offer a "magic bullet" that will be the answer to everything. Rather, it addresses the complex mix that allows a church to become healthy, mission oriented, growing and reproducing. I think King's Church represents a kind of urban church of the future showing that it is possible to have an impact in the great urban multi-ethnic cities of the world in spite of the obstacles often encountered in leadership, finance, land and government relationships. Reading this book will expand your faith in what God can do and give you ideas on how to work that faith out.'

Steve Nicholson – Senior Pastor of Evanston Vineyard, USA and Church Planting Task Force Director for the Vineyard movement, USA

'Steve Tibbert has overseen remarkable church growth during the last 15 years. He is a church leader with much to teach us.'

Nicky Gumbel – Vicar of Holy Trinity Brompton, London, author and developer of the Alpha Course

'Steve Tibbert has written us an important book full of practical leadership lessons to help all of us who have responsibilities in the church. Whilst remaining down to earth, it inspires us to see churches grow for the sake of reaching unbelievers with the good news and demonstrating the glory of God in diversity.'

David Devenish – Elder of Woodside Church, Bedford, and member of the International Leadership Team for Newfrontiers

GOOD TO GROW

Building a missional church in the 21st Century
– one church's story

STEVE TIBBERT WITH VAL TAYLOR

Authentic

Copyright © 2011 Steve Tibbert and Val Taylor

17 16 15 14 13 12 11   7 6 5 4 3 2 1

First published 2011 by Authentic Media Limited
Presley Way, Crownhill, Milton Keynes, MK8 0ES
www.authenticmedia.co.uk

British Library Cataloguing in Publication Data

A catalogue record for this book is available from the
British Library

ISBN-13: 978-1-86024-812-2

Cover design by Paul Airy at DesignLeft (www.designleft.co.uk)
Printed and bound in Great Britain by Cox and Wyman, Reading

CONTENTS

To Deb – love of my life.
Thanks for coming on the adventure and being
my best friend: we have walked each step of this
journey together.

And to Ben, Josh and Sam – three excellent
young men.
Keep serving God!

Acknowledgements

The making of a leader is a journey which, as it involves many people and varied experiences, is difficult to summarize briefly. If I have missed anyone, please forgive me.

I am extremely grateful to my parents for both a Christian foundation and a great example. Dad – thanks for being an outstanding leader in your generation and for the ongoing advice and counsel. If anyone has discipled me in leadership, you have. Mum – thanks for providing a great home to grow up in and for increasing my blog hits! Martin – thanks for being a great brother and friend.

Peter Ledger was the first to give me a leadership opportunity. Thanks for investing in me: much I have implemented at King's has its history in your leadership.

Ron Hopgood – thanks for covering my back when I was a young man starting to lead his first church. Phil Varley – thanks for being my friend: our friendship and partnership is at the heart of the King's story. Paul Braithwaite – for your friendship, counsel and commitment, my thanks. We would not be where we are without your contribution.

Steve Nicholson – thanks for taking time to invest in the church at King's: you have mentored me more than you realize.

Terry Virgo – thanks for providing the apostolic environment and pioneering the values upon which King's Church is built. It is a huge privilege to be caught up with your mission. The times of prayer, whether in your home or on numerous other occasions, have been truly inspiring. In your passion for Jesus and his church you are a model worth following.

Dave Holden, David Devenish, David Stroud, Lex Loizides, Brian Watts – all good friends and influences on my life, ministry and church – my thanks.

Joel Virgo, David Misselbrook, Mark Landreth-Smith and Guy Miller – thanks for giving time to read and comment on the original draft. The book is better for your help.

Val Taylor has been my co-writer. As I left school at 16 with no exams and dyslexic tendencies, such involvement is the reason why this book is readable. Thank you! And to Carol Ashley-Smith, who is an outstanding PA – in the midst of everything else you cover, thanks for your help with the research for this book.

To those who have served King's – on the eldership, as trustees and as part of the staff team – thanks for serving his church with such dedication.

And to the people of King's – this is our story. To those who were here when we arrived fifteen years ago, thanks for taking a risk on a young man . . . and if you have joined our journey since, you are part of a great church to serve and lead. I thank God for all of you!

Introduction – Looking Back

While working on the later chapters of this book, I received a long-awaited call from our solicitor to confirm the completion of the purchase of an additional building – one we had been pursuing for over a year. This extensive former language college was now ours. God is good!

Acquiring a large facility was something I had always thought would be the privilege of only a large provincial church, primarily because of the cost and the shortage of available land in London. On hearing that the building was now ours I was excited and relieved, but also had a clear-eyed understanding that we were now committed to a multimillion-pound building project. While the building 'only' cost £3.5 million to buy, when the refurbishment was complete the project would probably exceed £6 million.

September 1995 seems a long way back – the Tibbert family had first arrived in London, and a young, inexperienced leader had inherited a small band of hurting believers occupying an old building that needed significant renovation. Together we began a journey which has led us to this moment. This book tells our story. My hope is that it will encourage and equip many to believe God for all he has for his church and their nation.

The start of yet another new phase in our church life is an ideal point to take stock and look at the journey that has brought us to this crucial time – yet another crucial time – in the life of King's and in my own ministry. This book seeks to follow in the tradition of leaders like Moses who, when the people were about to enter the Promised Land, took them through their history in God, giving them faith and focus for the future (Deuteronomy 32). I hope that some of what I will recount here will help other leaders in the task of building the church. It's a task worth giving your life to.

This book is mainly about how to grow a church, and the leadership challenges that growth brings. Gathering a crowd is easy to do – just host a rock concert or a sporting event or take a trip to a theme park. The same can be true in church life. I recently attended a church which had a huge crowd, many times bigger than the church I lead, but the gospel preached was full of 'prosperity theology' – an appealing doctrine in a materialistic culture, but not the gospel as I understand it. Behind the growth in numbers at King's we must ask the qualitative questions, those concerning maturity, discipleship, holiness and Christlikeness – even if these are less easy to quantify.

King's Church is situated in Catford in south-east London and is part of the Newfrontiers family of churches founded by Terry Virgo. We are part of a movement on a mission together. A recent blog posting by Adrian Warnock expresses its beginnings well:

Terry Virgo founded Newfrontiers back in the mid 1970s. He was church planting before it was cool. He formed a missional network before the phrase was coined . . . Most of these churches began as house churches. But many have grown to become warehouse churches.

(adrianwarnock.com)

And I would add that this is a movement held together by apostolic ministry.

Some of the key biblical values that shape us are Grace, Church, Word, Spirit, Worship, Mission, Faith, Community, the Poor, Prayer and Relationship. King's Church has benefited enormously from our partnership with Newfrontiers – the network is far from perfect, but we are learning together, theologically and in practice. Church growth is not all about numbers – it's about an individual being found by God and transformed into a disciple of Jesus. We aim to 'present everyone mature in Christ' (Col. 1:28, ESV). As Bill Hybels, who leads Willow Creek Community Church in the USA, has put it so well – 'The Kingdom of God advances one life at a time.'

My personal history in God began with the heritage of a Christian home. From the age of eight I had attended Brickhill Baptist Church in my home town of Bedford, UK, at first rather grudgingly with my parents and then mostly through my involvement with the Boys' Brigade, which provided my first real experience of leadership (I made it to sergeant!). The girls in the youth group were the other attraction – the church and Christ himself seemed irrelevant.

Then, through the death of a friend in a motorbike accident, I began a journey which resulted in faith. It was in Brickhill Church that I was saved and baptized, and married a beautiful girl from the youth group called Deb. Our two oldest sons, Ben and Josh, were born there and it was the first place that I preached. Afterwards, the comment of Peter Ledger, the pastor and one of my fathers in Christ, was that it was 'a bit loose at the seams'. I was 21 and preaching to a 300-member church – in hindsight a rare privilege and providing excellent first leadership lessons, namely 'give youth a chance' and remember that initial fruit is secondary to long-term development.

The church survived my first preach – and many more after that. I led worship at the biggest outreach event of the year, the Christmas carol service, and also headed up the youth work and the twenties group. At around the age of 22 I was invited to attend the elders' meetings – an opinionated, arrogant, outspoken young man with much to say and far more to learn – but I was passionate for God and his church, and I still am.

Five years later, married to Deb, I left a successful job in sales and marketing to become youth pastor at Brickhill, swapping my generous salary and BMW for a lot less money and my sister-in-law's old Ford Fiesta 950L with eighty thousand miles on the clock. I believed then, as now, that money is nothing compared to eternity – self-leadership at that stage was more instinctive than understood; youthful passion was the order of the day rather than considered conclusions.

The next five years were exciting and fulfilling. They included being asked to head up youth ministry in Newfrontiers, speaking to and leading 1,500 young people at Stoneleigh Bible Week – another example of being thrown in at the deep end and surviving to tell the story. Many of the lessons that I learned in those formative years have shaped my ministry more than I can express in a few sentences – I'm extremely grateful to Peter Ledger and the eldership team at Brickhill at that time, who allowed me to experiment. I hope that on reflection they will consider the trust they placed in me was worth the risk and a good investment.

I was settled where I was – in fact as Peter approached 60 I dreamed of leading Brickhill, the only church I had experienced. It seemed a logical step, but God had other plans. The church entered a troubled time, with Peter becoming ill and painful decisions having to be made in the leadership.

I found myself facing a future that involved leading a church in a town somewhere else. The prospect was both exciting and scary at the same time – but the call of God was clear. Deb was immediately supportive – her two comments were, 'I trust your lead' and 'I'll go anywhere but London . . .'

A year later we were driving away from our home town, our families and our friends to begin leading a church in London. Reflecting on the preparation I received at Brickhill and how God used pain and conflict to move us on, I'm grateful that he did, for otherwise the lessons since learned and the story of King's Church that follows would never have happened . . .

Steve Tibbert
September 2010
www.stibbertleadership.blogspot.com
www.kingschurchlondon.org

1995–2000:

Two Hundred to Three Hundred

A Prophetic Foundation

King's Church was formed when two churches (Catford Hill Baptist and Allerford Church) felt God speaking to them about joining forces. Following an exciting start with over 300 people coming together, the church went through a difficult period, which meant that when Deb and I arrived the size had shrunk by 50 per cent and the church building at Catford Hill was in a state of disrepair – when it rained the roof leaked.

All leaders inherit the same things from the past – the positives *and* the problems. We inherited an extremely well-taught church, for which I have had good reason to be very grateful. A healthy church is well taught and well led. In my experience the reason why most churches aren't growing is that they are under-led. In a situation where there is no growth the lead elder often defaults to his primary gift – he may conclude that he needs to teach more. The additional preaching load

> In my experience the reason why most churches aren't growing is that they are under-led.

and preparation time then reduces his leadership capacity.

This in no way plays down the importance of good teaching, but rather highlights the importance of good leadership in making a church grow and flourish. As Bill Hybels once said, 'It is difficult to lead well and speak well in the same week' – leaders of growing churches seem to be able to excel in both and know at any given point where they need to prioritize. Those who had gone before me had laid a good foundation, resulting in a core of people extremely well taught and committed to Christ. Whenever I have had the pleasure of meeting my predecessors they have always been very encouraging to me – to John Colwell and Richard Haydon-Knowell I say, 'Thank you. This is your story too.'

Revelation

'Do not treat prophecies with contempt. Test everything. Hold on to the good' (1 Thess. 5:20–21).

I had been leading the church for just four weeks when my friend and one of my mentors, Steve Nicholson (a Vineyard pastor from Chicago), visited the church with a prophetic team. Many of the leadership lessons I share in this book have the mark of Steve on them. There is no doubt of the significance of this first visit.

Steve and the team brought a series of prophetic pictures. We believed that these word pictures were from God – revelation to us that would help us understand who we were, who he is, and what he wanted us to do, for his glory and the blessing and health of his church.

Each one then needed an interpretation and an application. This is the record we have of the pictures from those team members:

- First, a military snare-drum, infantry division, early nineteenth century. The drum and some drumsticks – the sticks are slightly damaged. They are on a shelf in a basement, next to a window. They are slightly illuminated.
- That picture was burned away by the flame of a candle. The candle is in the second picture. It is in a darker, deeper basement. The candle is set down by a monk-type figure – a monk's cloak. A book, an old book, very ancient, dusty.
- Thirdly, I saw a church building which I took to be yours. Water had drained from the church into a gutter along the street and was running down into the drain, down into a deeper spot, and then it was just settling there.

Interpretation

After the prophetic word had been spoken the interpretation was brought: 'I saw a church building which I took to be yours. Water had drained from the church into the gutter along the street and was running down into the drain down into a deeper spot and then just settling there.'

When this word was given, three days previously someone had put a pickaxe through a pipe – and though it was not generally known, water was still running down the outside of the building as he spoke. This really got our attention – it was that remarkable. He went on:

> I think that I sometimes see drums when the Lord is trying to speak to me about messages like the call to battle: rhythms that keep the ranks going in battle. For your church there is a call, a vision that has been left aside a little bit. No one was playing it. The drums are what were taking the infantry forward.
>
> I think the candle speaks of the same thing. Something in the history of this church that the Lord wants to be redis-covered. In praying it through, as I see it – a positive thing – search in the history.

Application

When we delved into our church archives we found that one of C.H. Spurgeon's protégés had planted our church in Catford in 1880 – with a vision for a thousand mem-bers. This discovery came through a prophetic word – and it was in response to that that we outlined our vision to believe for that thousand-member church. It was, we believed, God 'reactivating' that vision of C.H. Spur-geon's in our day and it required an active response of faith from us as a church.

Our story is rooted in this prophetic word – it was God's 'now' word to us: a dream of a thousand-member church. It seemed a long way off, but only four weeks into our time in Catford God spoke so clearly – what an amazing God we serve. The difference between present reality and prophetic promises can be challenging. The contrast between future hope and present reality was clearly visible.

I found the first few months at King's demanding. Each Sunday morning I would begin with the call to worship, which always included an invitation to stand and worship God. By the end of the first song 80 per cent of the congregation would be sitting down – they had been through such a difficult period that the church had lost heart. 'Hope deferred makes the heart sick' (Prov. 13:12). The story of Adullam's cave from the Old Testament also came to mind – a place where the distressed and dejected gathered and David became leader of this dispirited band. I inherited an excellent group of people who were discouraged by what they had been through.

Added to this I had a personal struggle with the particular style of worship in use at that time – I felt that it needed a radical change, but how? We saw God provide in the shape of Phil Varley, a young musician who became a close friend. Deb and I invited him to come and live with us and further, to take a year out to serve God in the church. He accepted and is still at King's, having grown in gifts and responsibilities – he still heads up our worship teams, among all his other duties.

My patience with the worship group lasted four months, after which I asked all worship leaders, musicians and technical team members to stand down. During the same period I discovered that the consequences of an adulterous affair had not been handled well, requiring me to make a public statement to the church. The fellowship was also unaware of the financial state of the church – I called a meeting and communicated that information to them. Actually, the finances were healthier than many had believed in the absence of any facts to correct their fears, so on that issue, at least, there was great relief all round. These were difficult days and we felt as though we were on the mission field – and we were.

2

Building Mission-Focused Churches

At this point I feel I need to say something on the topic of mission focus in the church and deal with what I believe is an essential truth – that the church exists to grow. The Great Commission and the record of New Testament church experience together lead me to a deep conviction that normal church life includes gospel breakthrough. Such knowledge fuels my belief that mission is at the heart of all the church does and is.

I truly believe that mission must take centre stage in the life of a local church, and I am convinced that we must build mission-focused communities and avoid any separation between normal church life and our mission agenda. This historical separation has led to an increasingly pastoral church and a growing number of parachurch organizations and agencies which have arisen to fill a gap.

During a sabbatical in 2003 I looked at apostolic ministry in the books of the New Testament, examining them in the context of mission. Reading Thomas Schreiner's *Paul, Apostle of God's Glory in Christ* confirmed to me yet again that Paul wrote in a context of mission. I enjoyed retracing the steps of the apostolic bands through the book of Acts and the letters that were written in response to the challenge of embryonic churches being established. What a joy, with no deadline or the pressure of the next sermon hanging over me, to get an overview of this crucial time in the early church. What I read reinforced my understanding that the atmosphere of the New Testament is full of missionary zeal.

The promise of the Spirit in Acts 1 was given with the purpose of giving believers power to be witnesses in Jerusalem and in all Judea and Samaria and to the ends of the earth. When the Holy Spirit comes in Acts 2, Peter preaches the gospel; he does not focus on the manifestations or the fact that it made them feel good. Rather, we have Luke's wonderful summary phrase, 'and the Lord added to their number daily those who were being saved'. The Jerusalem-based church was full of evangelistic fervour.

The feel and atmosphere of the book of Acts is one of apostolic extension, new spheres of operation, gospel preaching, Spirit-empowered witness, church planting, signs and wonders, gospel breakthrough, times of huge challenge and progress – against the backdrop of persecution. This has been the testimony of the church through the generations and should be ours today. Elsewhere in the world we see churches of thousands and tens of thousands – this should be our expectation in our nation and all nations.

The missionary zeal of the New Testament should be experienced in everyday church life. As the prophet Isaiah says, 'It is too small a thing for you to be my servant to restore the tribes of Jacob and bring back those of

Israel I have kept. I will also make you a light for the Gentiles, that you may bring my salvation to the ends of the earth' (Isa. 49:6). This is about more than a quality of church life; it is about building churches that take the gospel into the local community and to the ends of the earth.

Out of my passion to build mission-focused communities has grown a deep concern about what I see as normal church life and mission. Where churches are led by those whose primary gifting is pastoral and teaching, the result is often a church that reproduces believers in that image. Mission becomes a secondary part of church life rather than a primary focus – something that was done in the past and that others do now. I believe this comes about in the following way. In the conditions I describe above, gifted, mission-focused leaders often leave the local church to join mission-focused organizations. The absence of such people within the central life of the church consequently pushes the church into an even more pastoral mode.

> **Where churches are led by those whose primary gifting is pastoral and teaching, the result is often a church that reproduces believers in that image.**

I agree with Howard Snyder, who said in his paper to the Lausanne Congress:

The church is the only divinely-appointed means for spreading the gospel . . . further, evangelism makes little sense, divorced from the fact of the Christian community . . . The evangelistic call intends to call persons to the body of Christ – the community of believers, with Jesus Christ as its essential and sovereign head.

Let's not settle for second-best. Let's build mission-focused churches so that together we can reach the nations.

To build mission-focused communities requires sustained, focused leadership in the local church – we must continue to take a close look at ourselves to ensure that we are practising what we preach. I find that local churches have a tendency to drift towards a pastoral mode, taking their agenda from believers rather than the lost.

> I find that local churches have a tendency to drift towards a pastoral mode, taking their agenda from believers rather than the lost.

During the last ten years of leading a local church based in south-east London, we have transitioned the church to ensure that mission is the primary drive in all we do. As a consequence, to our delight, we are seeing increasing numbers of people saved, and while I would love to report that we are seeing people saved and added daily, we can say that we are seeing someone saved and added, on average, every week.

To build mission-focused communities we need to continue to grow in our understanding of apostolic ministry. I heartily commend Dave Devenish's book *What on Earth is the Church For?* – a must-read. He brilliantly illustrates apostolic ministry as being not a static serving of churches but something where churches are caught up on mission together.

I love the passage in Romans 15:23–24 when Paul says, 'Since I have been longing for many years to see you, I plan to do so when I go to Spain. I hope to visit you while passing through and to have you assist me on my journey there.'

Already planning his next apostolic journey, Paul boldly suggests to a church he has never visited before that they should help him to get to Spain. We need to release and support those with clear apostolic gifting to help our churches to be pulled into the regions beyond our local reach. Our attitude should not be, 'How can we be served?' but rather, 'How can we serve?'

To build mission-focused communities we must make space for the gift of the evangelist to shape our church life. Lex Loizides, a leader from one of the Newfrontiers churches in South Africa, has helped me so much on this. On a recent visit he made to King's, we had planned a gospel healing meeting: I suggested forty-five minutes' worship and then about thirty minutes for preaching and response. Lex laughed at me and said graciously, 'Let's do it this way – twenty minutes' worship, then testimony, words of knowledge,

> To build mission-focused communities we need to ensure that we identify, recruit and train leaders to have mission focus and skills.

prayer for the sick, preach the gospel, make an appeal, prayer for the sick again.' With all my desire to see gospel breakthrough, I had planned a meeting for believers!

To build mission-focused communities we need to ensure that we identify, recruit and train leaders to have mission focus and skills. Our training programmes should continue to be flexible in achieving our goal. Interestingly, Professor Leslie J. Francis summarizes his article in *Quadrant* magazine by saying, 'Once . . . ministry in the UK becomes reconceptualized in terms of growing new churches . . . then the leadership qualities prized by the churches' selection criteria may also need to be revisited' (*Quadrant*, January 2006). I could not agree more.

We still have much to learn – I sense that in the coming days we may see a shift in relationship between what are called para-church organizations and new church movements such as Newfrontiers. We still have much to learn from the vast experience of such agencies in specialist areas, knowledge attuned to various other cultures, gained over decades of faithful service. I believe we will increasingly see a partnership aspect to this relationship – with churches drawing on that experience as we send people out to plant new churches across the globe.

In conclusion, I believe we must continue to look to a biblical model of church which in no way separates local church life and mission. Mission-based organizations have sprung into life in reaction to local mission impotence, but I would argue that the result has been to weaken churches rather than solving the

> Mission-based organizations have sprung into life in reaction to local mission impotence.

problem, making the church more pastoral as a result. The lasting benefit of such mission is limited because when evangelistic fruit ends up in local churches, and these are weak, then weak disciples will be produced. As David Watson says in *I Believe in Evangelism*, 'If we fail to build individuals into the corporate life of the church we have missed the purpose of evangelism; it is one thing to reap, it is another to disciple and add.'

The local church must make the Great Commission central to its agenda. We must lift our eyes to the harvest field and truly model an integrated strategy of reaching the lost, caring for the poor and training and sending leaders, with such generosity that many who have given up on the church will return.

God is looking for such communities to emerge in our generation. Let's build them, to his glory!

3

Your History Shapes You

In my first few months at King's Church, I decided that my top priority was to get to know everyone. This involved many Sunday lunches with people in the church – everyone was extremely welcoming. It was an opportunity to build some friendships and understand the recent history of the church. I believe that before you initiate any change, understanding the history of the people you are leading is extremely important. History shapes both individuals and churches more than most people realize.

> History shapes both individuals and churches more than most people realize.

It's vital for an incoming pastor to know the history of the church he is going to lead. What has shaped it over recent years? What important events have occurred (both successes and the failures)? What type of ministry has brought about the recent vision of the church? While there are positive legacy issues to be grateful for, what negative legacy issues still require attention?

What prophetic words have influenced the church? All these elements help to shape a church and will contribute to the agenda for the future. Even as an individual, the path you have taken to get where you are will often define your thinking. To be aware of this is crucial; knowing the formative elements in your development is an important part of self-awareness.

If you want to know yourself, know your history. A trivial but revealing example of this for me would be what happened when Deb and I got married, with the wedding gift list. Deb and her mum compiled the list – I stayed well clear of the process until it was nearly done and Deb suggested that I have a look to see if there was anything I wanted to add. I went through it and – in all seriousness – said to Deb, 'Where's the trolley?'

'Trolley? What trolley? What do you want a trolley for?'

'The one that sits in the kitchen, where we put the newspapers so we know where they are when we want them. And when we have a family do or Sunday tea, the trolley comes out to the living room with the tea and sandwiches.'

My mum had a trolley in her kitchen and guess what? So did my Nana! And when we went to visit and had tea, out would come the trolley. (Anyone relating to this story?) So of *course* I asked, 'Where's the trolley?'

Deb said to me, quite firmly – more firmly than I thought necessary, really – 'We are *never* having a trolley in our house.'

I've learned that your upbringing, your history, shapes you. Sometimes we're in reaction to it – for me this would be the formal stuff that goes with ministry.

When I first came to King's I was in reaction to what is now known within King's as 'Pastor on the Door' duty, where at the end of each meeting the pastor stands at the main exit and says goodbye to everyone as they leave. For five years after we came no one performed that task. Then another elder volunteered to cover it, and when he began to pick up on visitors and new people, making a link with them, I suddenly saw the value of such a 'duty' and recognized my mistake in living in reaction to my past experience.

Sometimes the past provides a model that we respond positively to and use for reference, or we even just assume 'that's the way to do it' in a particular area. As you become older you learn that your history shapes you more than you realized before – I'm certainly finding this. Into your adulthood and marriage you bring your own upbringing and the examples of your parents – good and bad. I would suggest that it is important to be aware of how your history has shaped you – and especially what you are in reaction to.

After a few months' grace I came under increasing pressure to change almost every area of church life. We needed to sort out the children's ministry, the home groups and the prayer life of the church – to name but a few. Expectations were high, trust in leadership was low, and everyone had a view on where we should start.

I realized I needed a plan and a way to prioritize the many challenges we faced. This would provide a focused framework for us at leadership level and also help to manage expectations in the church. We identified five areas of church life for review:

1. Sunday worship meetings – style and content
2. Leadership team – composition and structure
3. Finance and giving
4. Mission – establishing a church culture
5. Buildings and facilities – condition and size

This brought some shape to the first year, and in doing this I stumbled (yet again) on a leadership strategy to deal with major change. Highlighting selected areas for review announced the intention that there would be change in these areas and so gave permission for changes to occur. The counsel and support of Dave Holden, who was overseeing the church, was invaluable at this time.

> Highlighting selected areas for review announced the intention that there would be change in these areas and so gave permission for changes to occur.

The first months continued to be demanding – each Sunday that I preached, one member saw it as his job to critique my sermon, mentioning how in the Greek it said this or that. After a while I encouraged him to find another church where the sermons fitted his interpretation of scripture – I found out later he joined a local Baptist church and at the local ministers' fraternal I heard how he continued to provide a weekly critique of that minister's sermons.

Home life was demanding – we had two young sons, our second one didn't sleep through the night for over a year, and we had no grandparents near, or long-standing immediately accessible friendships, to give support. A number of people in the church were helpful at this period – now we recognize the cost to them of this support. This stage of life could be neatly summed up by the occasion in late 1995 when we pulled up outside our house in our car. Realizing that both Ben and Josh were asleep in the back, Deb and I looked at each other and said, 'Let's just stay in the car for a while . . . ' It was 5 o'clock on a Sunday afternoon and we both dozed off too. Anyone walking by would have witnessed this scene of the whole family asleep in the car – we laugh about it now, but it shows just how physically tired we were.

4

Issues of Character

It became increasingly clear to me that the previous ten years of decline in the church had left their residue of failure, so before we could look to the future we needed to address the past. I decided to tackle it head on through speaking on a Sunday about 'Churches and Leaders that Fail' – using Mark's Gospel and the stories of Jesus feeding four thousand and then five thousand people. It was as if Jesus had to repeat this fantastic miracle because the disciples hadn't learned the principle he was teaching them the first time round. This seemed an important moment in our church life as we tried to gain momentum. I prepared hard, and when Sunday arrived I was ready.

The worship went well. I stood up to give a few notices before preaching, and as I looked out at the people I saw John Colwell, my predecessor, sitting in the congregation. My heart sank. How could I possibly address this important subject with the previous pastor right in front of me? And I wondered – what would he make of my preaching? I was still learning the art – as I still am – and John was now lecturing at Spurgeon's

College, a brilliant teacher and a biblical scholar. I was young and inexperienced, and I definitely felt it at that moment.

I did the notices on 'auto pilot' – in my mind (and stomach) I was trying to find a way out. Should I change the message, or soften the prophetic punch and application? The decision was made in a few seconds of reflection. God had given this message, and it was my task to deliver it. The fear of men too often cripples leaders. I delivered the message, trusted God and went for it.

There are many such leadership moments which you cannot learn in a college or even from a book like this on leadership – this is all about what goes on inside a leader's heart, mind and gut. The external challenges of leadership and the internal challenges go hand in hand. Leadership is far more than clever techniques or the latest ideas; it is much more about what goes on internally in a leader's heart and mind. To say it straight – it takes courage. You could say it was my 'Joshua moment', my call to be strong and very courageous (Josh. 1:7). As is often the case, it seems a small thing now, but at the time it was huge.

Obviously, failure in leadership and church life is not just addressed in one sermon, or even in a series, but we began the journey of regaining trust,

> There are many such leadership moments which you cannot learn in a college or even from a book like this on leadership – this is all about what goes on inside a leader's heart, mind and gut.

a vital ingredient in any form of leadership. This was an important moment for the church – and it turned out to be an even more important moment for me.

It is easy to forget that first year and all its hard work when you have not stopped growing for over a decade since, but in the first twelve months (from 1995 to 1996) we saw no growth. The building was in a poor state, and not everyone was happy with my idea to ask all the musicians, worship leaders and sound engineers to stand down – one family left the church over that call. After that, Phil Varley (now our executive pastor and head of our worship team) and I led worship for a year together.

We began to consider doing the Alpha course rather than the regular Saturday morning outreach in the town centre, which had seen little or no fruit. Money was tight. I began to work on the transition of the leadership team, a group of twelve people I had inherited – brilliant people, but not all of them were leaders and it was far too big a group to function effectively. I am delighted to report that nine of that twelve are still attending King's, another became a full-time pastor in America, and my dear friends Paul and Charlotte Braithwaite, now living in France, are still involved, even at a distance. Their love for King's, along with Paul's wonderful gifts, has resulted in him being actively involved in our current building project. More of that later.

After a few months at King's, one day I went up to central London, where Paul worked, so we could have lunch together. I was meeting with all the leadership team members individually, building friendship and trying to discover the gift and passion of each one. When I asked Paul about his gift, he replied, 'I'm not really sure what my gifts are, but my greatest strength is loyalty.' Paul later joined the full-time staff team and served as an elder for several years before relocating to France. We still speak on the phone most days, and his remarkable capacity and insight have brilliantly served me and the church here at King's – more than most people know. He is truly a man of his word. Loyalty is a critical component of leadership – it should be highly valued and is a precious deposit of trust. It is something way beyond a matter of employment. Members of a team live with each other's idiosyncrasies and those of the team leader – loyalty is realistic about those foibles, strengths and weaknesses and continues to support and promote the highest good of the church, the leader and the other team members. It is a wise leader who strives to be worthy of such loyalty.

> Loyalty is a critical component of leadership – it should be highly valued and is a precious deposit of trust.

Such character issues are not just a matter for team members. The quality of a leader's character is always going to be a major influence on the outcome of that life and ministry. Personality and gifting will influence the impact, but ultimately it's godly character and investment in developing that character that will give depth and integrity to what is achieved. Self-awareness, recognizing one's own shortcomings and limitations in this area, as well as strengths, gives a young leader the chance to come before God and ask for his grace to grow in character. At the same time, it requires humility to seek advice and mentoring from those who show character traits to aspire to – but such an investment will pay dividends, now and in eternity.

5

A Mission Philosophy

At this stage I also began to express what I would now call a *philosophy of ministry*. In my experience most conflict within teams comes through a clash over the philosophy of ministry rather than a clash of personalities or biblical values – or even doctrine. A philosophy of ministry emphasizes how a value is worked out or the priority it is given over another value in any church setting.

Which is more important: to be pastoral as a church, or missional? Which should come first when allocating resources? Both are biblical values, but which should take priority?

> In my experience most conflict within teams comes through a clash over the philosophy of ministry rather than a clash of personalities or biblical values – or even doctrine.

In our history the clash over inclusivity and quality caused more pain than nearly any other subject. There were those who were happy to sacrifice quality in order to include anyone who wanted to be involved in a particular ministry or event. Then there were others, including me, who, while wanting to involve many people, at the same time wanted to retain high quality in all we did. Everyone wanted both to a certain extent, but team members prioritized them differently. A good example of this would have been in the area of our corporate worship and musicianship. This led to diverging definitions of success for those members within the team and in the church – conflict was inevitable.

'Philosophy of ministry' also includes how you choose to work out a biblical value. Most Christians agree we should share our faith, but the ways are numerous – from going door to door to 'barbecues for Jesus', to 'hellfire preaching', to an approach

> At King's we operate on the principle of taking people on a journey, accepting them at their own starting point and inviting them to come on that journey of discovery.

that is relational and slow, and to the Alpha course. What do you emphasize? At King's we operate on the principle of taking people on a journey, accepting them at their own starting point and inviting them to come on that journey of discovery. We are 'attractional' in our programming and 'incarnational' in our equipping, encouraging our believers to witness in the workplace, in the college or at the school gate.

You need an agreed philosophy of ministry in every area of church life – worship, counselling, pastoral care, leadership, budgeting, etc. in order to avoid tensions.

At this point, once again, acting more out of instinct than considered reflection, I began to teach the church on the principle of becoming primarily a *missionary* church rather than being a *pastoral* church. I recognized that we were taking our own people on a journey. This was another good example of the need to be aware of the history when taking the church through transition. We were beginning to teach and lead the church into the future. Teaching from David Devenish – an influential leader from one of the Newfrontiers churches in Bedford – and a book by Robert Warren called *Building Missionary Congregations* were very useful as resource materials at that time. In that book Robert Warren states:

> At the heart of the distinction . . . between a pastoral and a missionary church is the difference between a church organised around sustaining, developing and promoting its own life, and a church organised around participating in God's mission in the world to establish his redemptive purposes in the whole of human life. A working definition of a missionary congregation is thus:
>
> A missionary congregation is a church which takes its identity, priorities and agenda from participation in God's mission in the world.

Churches quickly reflect the passion and gifting of the lead pastor. The church I had inherited had a very good biblical foundation, reflecting the gift mix of my predecessor. I was glad of this, but I was now more interested in reaching London with the gospel of Jesus Christ than with just having a well-taught church.

> **Churches quickly reflect the passion and gifting of the lead pastor.**

Rather than becoming an accumulation of information, good teaching leads to mission. As Paul puts it in Philippians 4:9, 'Whatever you have learned . . . put it into practice.'

I once thought I was an evangelist, until I met one, but I have always been a leader with a passion for the lost, whether in leading a Bible study group for work colleagues, running a non-alcoholic bar as a youth pastor, or just sharing my faith one to one. While not original in outlook, this was over a decade before the 'missional' outlook from church leaders in the USA such as Tim Keller and Mark Driscoll caught our attention. In fact the suggested growth engine of the day was the cell church movement, with Bill Beckham and others. We did not go in that direction, as I believed that in the order of priority of things that needed urgent attention at King's, sorting out the small group system was *way* down the list. Too often church leaders are looking for a solution to help their church to grow – the latest idea, a golden bullet, one size fits all. My experience is that church life is more complex: we need a whole range of things to come together in order to be effective.

In his book *Natural Church Development*, Christian Schwarz refers to a teaching aid he uses when speaking to church leadership teams. He calls it 'the minimum barrel' – a tub with staves (the upright wooden 'ribs' of the barrel) of varying lengths. Each stave represents a quality characteristic of the church, and its length is determined by its strength within the church. Examples would be 'structures' or 'passionate spirituality'. The tub is then filled with water, which represents those attending the church. At some point the water begins to escape from the barrel and is lost – and the place where the loss occurs is determined by the minimum factor, the weakest point.

Every analogy breaks down at some point, and there may be other factors to take into consideration, but this is a useful picture to help us recognize that we need to have the courage to take on a rigorous examination of our church life and work at strengthening our weak places. If God is blessing us by pouring in new people, we do not want to waste what he has given by inattention to where leakage occurs.

> If God is blessing us by pouring in new people, we do not want to waste what he has given by inattention to where leakage occurs.

In his book *The Purpose Driven Church*, Rick Warren has a useful diagram (see opposite page) that I have found instructive. This diagram has become part of my own thinking about the church's mission in the world.

Although most people's eyes are drawn into the centre of the diagram, where the core group exists, I prefer to start with the outer rim. Where the rings represent 'unchurched, regular attenders, members, maturing members, core lay ministers' you could as easily put the following – 'mercy, mission, members, maturity, ministry'. What happens in the inner circles must begin with a focus on the outer edge and those lost people for whom Christ died.

Such thinking means that we inevitably link our mission with our programme. The strategy is that mission impacts our Sunday programme, which is connected to our midweek events – for example, we may plan a baptismal service to take place just before the launch of the next Alpha course.

6

Momentum and Vision

'Momentum makes leaders look better than they are' (*The 21 Irrefutable Laws of Leadership*, John Maxwell).

This is true. I would say with no hesitation that I look a better leader than I am, because of momentum. In January 1997 something began to happen at King's Church: after fifteen months of seemingly fruitless work, we started growing. Nothing spectacular, but it was progress nevertheless – a small breath of momentum.

> I would say with no hesitation that I look a better leader than I am, because of momentum.

Since that time we have grown every year – on average at about 10 per cent and on two occasions at an amazing 25 per cent. But it started small, with a net growth of twenty people in one year. Growth has shaped my prayer and planning for the last fifteen years. *'Please Lord, 10 per cent growth!'* If you grow at 10 per cent every year for seven years you will double in size over the period – King's grew from two hundred to five hundred in ten years, then from five hundred to a thousand in another five years. If we continue to grow at a rate of 10 per cent per annum, in another seven years we look to be two thousand. As I write, we stand at an average Sunday attendance of over one thousand, so on this basis we find ourselves currently just ahead of the projected curve. It's important to remember that all journeys start with a small step: ours started in January 1997 with twenty extra people.

Also in January 1997, we began to set annual goals to track progress. I found this extremely helpful, both for our leaders and for the church. As a rule I set them at a level that is easy to achieve. I remember hearing a church leader saying that he was praying for his church to double in size in the next year. I did not believe him, and probably no one else did, but Christians are nice people, so we smiled sweetly and thought maybe God would do it – but it didn't happen.

At King's I was keen to continue to build trust in the leadership for the church, so I set annual goals which were achievable. I was confident we would reach them in a year's time and I have always worked on the basis that it is better to overachieve than to underachieve – even falling short by a small amount brings disappointment. This is where 'vision' is different to 'goals' – our vision has no timeline on it, our goals do.

We had taken some first steps, but major challenges still lay ahead. In September 1997, two years after arriving, I stood before the church – those still with us and a handful of new people – and presented our vision statement. To be honest, the outline was taken straight from

Rick Warren's book *Purpose Driven Church* – I just changed a few words, and of course adjusted the number from twenty thousand down to one thousand members!

I have had very few sleepless nights in my time in ministry. In those early days, exhaustion from life around our young children provided enough reason to sleep through the night, but on this occasion, in the weeks before the Vision Sunday, I was restless. Once again an internal challenge was happening – did I have faith to believe for a thousand-member church? To be honest, I was reasonably confident in my leadership ability to make it to five hundred members – that may seem arrogant, but is probably not an unrealistic reflection of the prophetic words on my life, my training to that point and the context of a city with eight million people. But a thousand members seemed to be in territory which was out of sight. In the end, I concluded that the prophetic word from Steve Nicholson and his prophetic team had led us to the thousand-member target – therefore a thousand it was, and if it ever did come to pass then people would know that this was a work of God, not of a particular leader.

Here is the vision statement that we adopted then. It is still clearly posted in the entrance to the King's Church Centre for all to see as they enter.

King's Church vision statement

In 1997, out of prophetic leading, we believe God gave us this vision for the church:

- It is a dream of a place where the hurting, the depressed, the frustrated and the confused can find love, acceptance, help, hope, forgiveness, guidance, encouragement and purpose.
- It is a dream of sharing the good news of Jesus Christ with thousands of residents in London.
- It is a dream of welcoming 1,000 members into fellowship in our church family made up of all generations and many nationalities.
- It is a dream of developing people to spiritual maturity, living out a life full of worship to the risen Lord Jesus.
- It is a dream of being a training centre, which will equip every believer for significant ministry and send many across the nation and the nations on short-term and longer-term mission.
- It is a dream of reproducing ourselves by planting at least one church every five years.
- It is a dream of having a facility which can serve our local needs, as well as serving regionally.

Steve Tibbert, Senior Pastor, September 1997

The overall response to the Vision Sunday was positive, but more than one faithful soul said I was living in cloud cuckoo land. But with a little growth momentum, and now something to reach for together, and with trust in leadership beginning to return, the foundation was set for another step forward. Not the small incremental step we anticipated, but what was to be a large leap of faith.

Vision, and clearly expressing that vision repeatedly, is a vital component in keeping the church moving forward. But this process needs to be handled with great

> Vision, and clearly expressing that vision repeatedly, is a vital component in keeping the church moving forward.

care. It is one thing to paint a picture of a preferred future – one that will help everyone to identify with that vision – but it is entirely another matter to deliver it. When a wise leader is setting vision, the key factor to be taken into account among the many that will clamour for his attention should be: what God has said. Further, that leader must understand the history of the church and what God has done and said before in its history, as well as having a sober assessment of his own gifts and capacity.

When sharing vision for the future of the church, or managing other change, I have found the following questions provide a helpful framework to enable others to get hold of that vision:

- Where are we?
- Where are we going?
- How are we going to get there?
- How can I be meaningfully involved?

On numerous occasions this set of questions has served the church well. There is a recognition within them that we need to face facts, we need to decide where we want to go, we need a plan to get there and we need to motivate others and provide manageable steps for them to have ownership and involvement in that plan.

At King's we not only have a vision statement but also a values statement, a mission statement and a statement of faith (see appendix). All of these have been crafted to clearly express what we are called to do (vision), what we practise (values), why we exist (mission) and what we believe (faith). I would maintain that clarity in these important areas is essential – for church leaders and for the people they serve.

7

The Important Triangle

Ron walked into my office. 'Steve, have you got five minutes? I think I've found a way to release £30,000 into our revenue.'

An excellent way to get my attention! An extra income stream into that part of our finances that maintains the normal life of the church, financing all our work among youth and children, pastoral care and our mercy ministries, would be really welcome. Ron explained that we had been claiming our tax refund from covenanted giving at the end of each financial year – effectively a year in arrears. He proposed that we claim this more regularly during the active financial year. It was a simple but effective idea and meant we would benefit from the one-off cash injection into the church income for the year 1997.

To create the momentum needed to get the church to continue with the first small steps in growth already made, we needed to increase the size of our staff. The King's staff team at that time consisted of Martin Alley (pastoral) and Ron Hopgood (administration and finance), both of whom worked full-time with me, and

Annie Twort (also pastoral) working part-time. That financial news from Ron resulted in the seed funding needed to take such a bold step and to increase the size of the team. It required our confidence that in a couple of years' time we could continue to fund the salaries of the staff we would take on and were committed to.

This is another example of a philosophy of ministry put into practice. It has been my practice to operate on the basis that we 'staff *for* growth' rather than *because* of growth. For good reasons, most churches that I know do the opposite, the rationale being 'We need more staff because we have grown.' It's a matter of asking the question: which comes first, the leadership capacity for growth or the leadership capacity to care for that growth? A mission-driven church is far more likely to staff for growth. The risks are higher but the commensurate rewards are greater. I'm glad to report that King's now sees people saved, on average, every week – I believe that the above approach has helped towards that result.

> We 'staff *for* growth' rather than *because* of growth. For good reasons, most churches that I know do the opposite, the rationale being 'We need more staff because we have grown.'

On that basis I invited my friend Howard Kellett to come to King's from the Sidcup church and lead our outreach team. He took over that work from me, also releasing me from leading the Alpha course. Howard had been working full-time as a school teacher up to this point; after four years at King's he went on to establish a successful new church in Manchester and is now leading a church plant in Cheltenham.

I had always believed that for King's to grow from two hundred people to five hundred we had to solve the *building* capacity problem and also increase the capacity of the full-time *team*. And we had to believe that God would provide enough money to achieve both simultaneously.

FACILITIES   FINANCE

TEAM

I have found this diagram to be a helpful tool which works with churches of any size. To recognize the correlation between team, building and money in enabling growth is vital. If a church has stopped growing, it is normally one of these issues, or a combination of them, which needs to be looked at carefully. It may help to explain why most churches never grow larger than two hundred.

> To recognize the correlation between team, building and money in enabling growth is vital.

In order to grow a church from two hundred to five hundred, first the leader of the church has to be able to lead in a completely different way to that previously used, primarily through other people. Rather than being the all-singing-all-dancing generalist, he has to transition to being a specialist team builder – less hands-on. The problem for some leaders is that at this point the very skills and gifts which have made the church grow to two hundred – their personal strengths – can become hindrances to going forward to the next stage.

Here's the likely problem. The existing pastor has seen the church grow from, say, fifty to 175. He loves the people and they love him – he is a good generalist and, as a skilled 'people' person, has built a strong community. Now, here's the challenge. These gifts could well limit further growth as he tries, for example, to maintain the same level of relational involvement with individuals which has been a keynote of his ministry. He needs to ask: am I willing to allow others to be 'hands on' with pastoring the flock? Do I have the skills to recruit, train and manage such a team? And he also needs to ask the crunch question – *will the church allow him to do this?*

With Phil Varley already on the team we had the leadership capacity to move things forward. While someone has to lead, the reality is that for anything of any substance to take place, it takes a team of committed and gifted men and women.

In his brilliant book *Good to Great*, Jim Collins observes that the good-to-great leaders began the transformation by first getting 'the right people on the bus (and the wrong people off the bus) and *then* figured out where to drive it.' Phil Varley is a great example of the right person being on the bus.

The downside to staffing for growth must be taken on board. If growth does not follow, you are likely to be unable to meet salary costs for the new team member. Good judgement as to when to step into a more pro-active approach to staffing is vital. As part of my own risk assessment for such a situation I always prepare an exit strategy for both the individual and the church. I don't consider this to be lack of faith, but good wisdom.

Also, at around the two hundred mark most churches face a facilities challenge: the building where they worship becomes full, and this requires a solution. Both the team enlargement and building capacity solutions require the leader to raise money – to fund new team members and at the same time to raise hundreds of thousands of pounds to solve the building limitations issue. The combination of these challenges can overwhelm the leader and produce a situation where the church is unable to continue growing. This was the challenge we were facing. At that time I thought that this was a once-in-a-lifetime challenge, but I discovered later that it happens again at around eight hundred people – but with more noughts on the end of the amount of money required!

8

A Personal Revelation

After my earlier experience when the eldership team at Brickhill got into difficulties, I was particularly sensitive to team dynamics. When I saw a two-day training course run by Peter Brierley from the company Christian Research called *Know Yourself, Know Your Team*, I thought it would be a useful and interesting couple of days' training – in fact it opened up for me a whole new world of thinking which continues to shape my leadership to this day.

Following those two stimulating days I invited Peter to do a day of training with my team, as part of which we all did a personality profile questionnaire. My test results confirmed that I was an extrovert, an external processor, with everyone hearing my thinking out loud – but they also revealed that I was a very intense person, not something to which I had given much thought. As I read that result I remember exclaiming aloud, 'That's not true!' – which made the rest of the team fall about laughing.

Once again, showing huge humility, I expressed to those present that they were all wrong, and went home from the day still absolutely convinced that I was actually a laid-back person. I walked into the kitchen at home and retold the events of the day. The conversation went something like this:

'Deb, you wouldn't believe what my personality test revealed today – I am an *intense* person! How wrong can that be? And also, d'you know what? The rest of the team actually agreed with that analysis!'

At this point Deb turned round and said, 'Steve, you are the most intense person I have ever met, and I should know – I'm married to you!'

That's what you call a show-stopper. I was hit for six, speechless – another first! I was 34 years old and had been in full-time ministry for seven years, had led a church for two years, had studied theology at a Bible college, had a reasonably successful business career, been married for eight years – but my level of self-awareness was way off the mark. How I viewed myself was very different to how others viewed me.

If I could dismiss the comments of the course trainers and my team, I could not avoid the words of my wife – and by the way, they were said with some conviction and passion. It has to be said that my idea of a good way to spend the first day of our annual family holiday was to initiate a review of our marriage and family life, including everything from our communication to our love life. The best and worst example of this was suggesting that on

> Most leaders have extremely low self-awareness and are unaware of how they process life and how others see them.

the first day of a French holiday we study *Recovering Biblical Manhood and Womanhood,* by John Piper and Wayne Grudem. All Deb wanted to do was sit by the pool and read a novel. Now I ask you, what would you prefer to do?

Most leaders have extremely low self-awareness and are unaware of how they process life and how others see them. This revelation initiated a time of sober reflection for me, and was the beginning of a journey of increased self-awareness which has helped me and my team cope with the challenges of communication and aided an understanding of different perspectives and personalities.

This greater awareness across the team – of how we all process life differently – has aided greater communication with each other. I never cease to be amazed at how five people in the same room can interpret the same conversation five different ways. I am convinced that good teams take time out from their normal work schedules to be 'upskilled' in interpersonal relationships and team dynamics. For our team this has proved to be generally fun – but we would all agree that at times it has proved very painful.

During that two-day course I was also introduced to the Belbin test. This is a secular test which allows you to discover your individual contribution to a team. This test helped me again, by giving me some

> I am convinced that good teams take time out from their normal work schedules to be 'upskilled' in interpersonal relationships and team dynamics.

understanding of my own strengths and so increasing my self-awareness even further – but probably more importantly it helped me to appreciate more those members of my team whose team contributions were different to my own. Too often leaders gather people around them who are exactly like them – like attracts like, as they say – but a well-rounded team is made up of those with completely different personalities and gifts. The role of the team leader is to maximize the potential in the room and keep the team together. I have always worked on the principle of 'know yourself and staff your weaknesses'.

For more information have a look at www.belbin.com.

I have since learned, through the input of Brian Watts, who pastors a church in Battersea and who is also an excellent coach in team work, that how the team members relate to each other and work together reflects how the church does the same. A look at the former will tend to give you a clear reading of the latter, especially when it comes to 'church temperature'. Signals from the team mirror what's happening in the church. This gives useful information to help you pastor people through change. A more recent example: when I found that one or two of the wives of King's leaders were beginning to feel isolated with the advent of the multiple meetings, this gave me the opportunity to address this issue for the whole church.

The diagram of a bicycle chain gives a useful picture here. What's happening with the smaller cog reflects what's happening in the larger wheel.

> How the team members relate to each other and work together reflects how the church does the same.

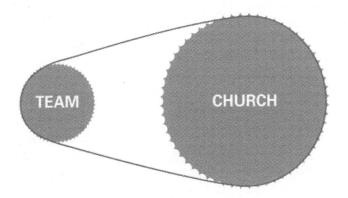

The team that exists at King's is becoming increasingly skilled. Self-awareness, understanding of team dynamics and the importance of the communication process both between team members and with the church as a whole – all of this is vital to the success of our church.

My favourite leadership quote of all time is from *Developing the Leaders Around You* by John Maxwell: 'Those closest to the leader determine the success level of that leader.'

The whole story of King's is one of team achievement and huge team effort. I have been surrounded by highly gifted, motivated people throughout the whole journey and I count it a privilege to work with this great team in one of the highest callings a person can have – to build the church.

9

KC2000

By 1998 King's Church had started to grow, but our Victorian building continued to present a major challenge. It was built in 1880 as part of C.H. Spurgeon's church planting endeavours in south London, but hardly any money had been spent on the facility in the intervening hundred years or so. It was limited in its capacity, with chairs that allowed seating for no more than 250 people 'comfortably', the toilets were old, the crèche room smelt of damp and the offices were located in a couple of Portacabins out at the back.

At leadership level we had been discussing what to do about the building. A number of options were considered, including a £250,000 refurbishment of the existing facility. I was up for something more radical – we needed not just a paint job but a building which could serve our vision in the coming years. Martin Heijne, an architect whose help and professional skill were to become important and integral factors in our future (Martin has now been involved in five building projects with us), produced plans based on a number of options. Unfortunately, because of the constraints of the size of our plot of land, none of them seemed to solve all the problems we faced, especially the need for a five-hundred-seat auditorium.

I showed the plans for the new project, named KC2000, to David Misselbrook. David and Ruth had been part of the church for a number of years and had played a vital role in keeping the church together during the difficult decade before my arrival. David was now about to shape the church for decades into the future. Taking a pencil, he began to draw on the paper plans in front of a small group of leaders. In that moment the kernel of an idea came into being, putting the new auditorium at the back of the building rather than the front, resulting in a significantly increased capacity.

All we needed to do was raise the £2 million required for the new building, get planning permission, agree an amended trust deed with our custodian trustees and sell two properties owned by the church – a smaller church building and a house elsewhere that King's still owned. At the age of 35 I embarked with the church on an amazing adventure of faith. I look back on it now: two hundred people and a young pastor – we were naive, mad, or hungry to see God work and see his vision fulfilled. Probably all three.

After the initial excitement our plans came to a screeching halt. Lewisham Council's Planning Department turned down our application for redevelopment. After agreeing the design and motivating the church to give, this came as a big blow. It was time to lead again. This involved taking further professional advice on how to successfully appeal against the decision, meeting up with all the local councillors to present our case, and finally and most importantly, calling the church to pray to ask God to overturn the decision. This roadblock to progress sent us back to God with the clear understanding that while human preparation and planning were important, nothing would happen unless we undergirded everything with prayer and sought his direction and intervention. This would continue to be the case, of course, at every stage of our story. A praying people in the hands of God can achieve a great deal. We placed great importance on the prayer life of the church, even moving the time of the prayer meeting from a Sunday evening to a midweek evening to maximize the attendance.

> This roadblock to progress sent us back to God with the clear understanding that while human preparation and planning were important, nothing would happen unless we undergirded everything with prayer.

Within a few months the planning officer we had been dealing with was assigned to another part of the borough, and I will never forget sitting in the old auditorium, with the new planning officer, Steve Isaacson, while Martin Heijne and I laid out our plans to redevelop the site. A number of months later I attended the Planning Committee meeting with councillors, planners and other officials, and our project was given the go-ahead.

I made many leadership mistakes during this period. Our plan to fund the development had assumed that if we were unable to sell the second church property we would be able to secure a bank loan against it. Six weeks before the building work was due to start, the highest offer to buy the property was from a religious sect – and under charity law, if we sold any property we were compelled to accept the highest offer. Then the bank, rather than lending us £250,000 and using the building as security at its full value, offered only £60,000 – so with a month and a half to go to the start of construction, without a loan from the bank we still had a £250,000 funding shortfall.

I remember the afternoon when Ron Hopgood, our church administrator, brought this information to me and the other leaders. This was not good news; the mood in the room was one of great disappointment. However, this was not a time to become depressed, this was a time for action.

An afternoon on the phone speaking to a number of friends in our network of churches gave me hope that we would be able to secure interest-free loans from them to cover the shortfall, but as we got into the detail I realized that £250,000 of loans needed to be secured against *something* – in other words, we could borrow that amount from other churches as long as we could find another £250,000 in security. All the tenders from construction companies came in above the level that our quantity surveyor had predicted, and with building costs rising at that time at a rate of 8 per cent a year, the project would soon move beyond us. Or we could accept the offer from the sect . . . It was decision time! What would you do?

I realized that if we did not make the jump now, we could get stuck for years to come, but I really did not want to sell the building to that particular group.

We decided to move ahead with the project and secure the interest-free loans of £250,000 against the homes of

Paul and Charlotte Braithwaite and Deb and me. We acted as guarantors – not something to do lightly, but I preferred that route to selling the Allerford church building to a group that I was not happy with. We remarketed the church building and about fifteen months later sold it to an Elim Pentecostal church at a higher price, making an additional £75,000 profit on the sale. And the gospel is still being preached from that location until this day. God is good!

Faith in God can be defined and described in many ways – on this occasion it felt like a huge leap. At any given time leadership requires wisdom and judgement which weighs the potential risks and then prayerfully and confidently steps into action. This was such a moment: one not without personal risk, but in my view this was the right option – and the only one to follow.

So we embarked on our first building project at King's. Deb and I, along with other committed people at King's, began to double-tithe. Yes – that's 20 per cent *before* tax. We relocated our offices off site in the Braithwaites' home, which was nearby, and moved our Sunday meetings into the local school hall – three meetings each Sunday, in order to get everyone in, as there was room for only one hundred each time. Of course I wasn't aware that some eight years later the newly extended building would also be used for three meetings each Sunday. But God knew, and so our time at the school was preparation for what was to come.

This season taught me a great deal about church leadership. Firstly and foundationally, prayer is powerful and some decisions are outside your control – only God can move planners to another job. Also, I learned many lessons on how to lead a church into a building project. As I reflect on this particular part of the journey, my advice to any church leadership entering into a building project would be as follows:

- Take legal advice and speak to banks *early*.
- Everything will always take longer than you expect.
- The project will always cost more than you are originally told.
- Keep the vision before the people.
- Build relationships with council officers.
- Ask advice from others who have gone down this path before.
- Visit other churches and see what they have done.

10

Building a Great Marriage

While building the full-time team at the church, Deb and I began to realize that as the church began to grow our marriage needed to grow in parallel. It has been my observation that sometimes the limiting factor of a ministry's effectiveness and sustainability has nothing to do with the leader's capacity or gift – or that of the team. A weak leadership marriage, rather than being a place of rest and refreshment, becomes a limiting factor, sometimes tragically derailing the whole deal. An important motto around King's would be: 'Let's not build a big church and lose a marriage.'

I believe it is critically important to build *great*

> Sometimes the limiting factor of a ministry's effectiveness and sustainability has nothing to do with the leader's capacity or gift – or that of the team. A weak leadership marriage, rather than being a place of rest and refresment, becomes a limiting factor, sometimes tragically derailing the whole deal.

marriages: these provide a strong foundation from which to serve God together. This vital partnership is worth investing in with time and energy. And to be honest, this is not a great hardship for me. Deb is the love of my life, so any excuse to spend time with her works for me, although I do meet leaders who seem to prefer to be 'doing ministry' to being at home. I made this mistake early on in our marriage. Young and ambitious, I would be out six nights a week – I see this now as my actions revealing my heart. This came to a head following a ministry trip to India which required me to leave on Christmas Day (yes, Christmas Day!).

While away on this ministry trip, I was already thinking about the next one – this was nine months before we moved to London. God spoke to me then – that I had not prioritized Deb enough. Upon my return I told Deb what God had said to me, repented of my previous attitude and practice and began a re-adjustment in my work/life balance. Putting Deb and the family above the demands of ministry required a major reordering of my priorities. This is an ongoing process and most of the time I think we have the balance about right now. That repentance opened a period of reflection about our marriage.

> The personal life of the leader and their corporate leadership are totally linked together.

In the first five years at King's, not only were we building a church, we were building a marriage that would provide a place of mutual support and rest – in order to achieve all God has called us to. The personal life of the leader and their corporate leadership are totally linked together, in my experience. Our culture has made a huge mistake in separating the private and the public. Integrity, whether in private life or public arena, is always an issue of character.

A Barometer for Your Marriage?

In his book *Sheet Music*, Christian psychologist Dr Kevin Leman tells couples wishing to improve the quality of their marriages: 'I spend a lot of time trying to help women get more active in the bedroom and trying to help men get active *everywhere else.*'

> Integrity, whether in private life or public arena, is always an issue of character.

Deb and I recently ran a Saturday morning seminar at King's for married couples, entitled 'Sex, Romance and God'. It was part of a broader teaching series we had been running on Sundays, called 'Sex in the City', based on 1 Corinthians. The seminar was for married couples only and gave us the opportunity to address the subject of sex and romance in marriage far more openly than would be appropriate on a Sunday morning. The seminar was both challenging and fun, and we were asked questions we have never been asked before. We had planned to hold the seminar on just one Saturday, but had to repeat it the following weekend to meet demand. It was superb to have so many couples seeking to improve the sex and intimacy in their marriages.

As we all know, sex is just one aspect of marriage. But an observation we have made during our years in pastoral ministry is that the quality of a couple's sex life is a good 'barometer' for the health of the marriage overall. If a couple are not communicating or are having problems in one part of their relationship, you can almost guarantee that that will quickly be reflected in the bedroom.

As part of the 'Sex, Romance and God' seminar, Deb and I spent some time looking at the different needs of men and women when it comes to maintaining intimacy in marriage. Gary and Barbara Rosberg, in their book *The 5 Sex Needs of Men and Women*, sum it up well:

> If a couple are not communicating or are having problems in one part of their relationship, you can almost guarantee that that will quickly be reflected in the bedroom.

> He (God) calls on men to connect emotionally with their wives in order to have their physical needs met; he calls on women to connect physically with their husbands in order to have their emotional needs met.

As a broad generalization (and there will always be exceptions), women need to feel emotionally connected in order to be physically intimate, whereas a man finds emotional connection through sex. Interestingly, men are wired in such a way that they are often more emotionally open after sex. Gary Rosberg says, 'Sometimes the best way to unlock a husband's emotions is through satisfying his physical need for sex.'

H. Norman Wright spells out these differences in this way:

For women, sex is only one means of intimacy out of many and not always the best one. For many men, sex is the only expression of intimacy.

Men tend to compress the meaning of intimacy into the sex act, and when they don't have that outlet, they can become frustrated and upset. Why? Because they're cut off from the only source of closeness they know.

Men are interested in closeness and intimacy, but they have different ways of defining and expressing it. (This) is an area where men and women need to talk, listen and understand the other person's . . . language. (Quoted in *The Christian Woman's Guide to Sexuality*, by Debra Evans)

11

Strengthening Your Marriage

It takes time and effort to build a great marriage, as well as the determination to ensure ministry priorities don't take precedence. In our experience so far, every time we have seen ministry breakthrough, our marriage has had to strengthen correspondingly. This has involved a commitment to talking openly about the challenges involved and being clear about what it means to continue to show love

> Every time we have seen ministry breakthrough, our marriage has had to strengthen correspondingly.

to each other. It is my belief that the strength of our marriage will have a direct impact on the effectiveness and potential of our ministry. For this reason, if no other, we should make a commitment to invest in our marriages.

A strong marriage is so important in ministry. There is so much at stake – if you fall morally, you can lose your wife, children, job and calling. Behind each story of a failed marriage there will be huge pain caused to families, churches and, most importantly, to God. I believe that our marriage commitment requires us to take some action to ensure we build a strong and healthy marriage.

Take responsibility for your marriage. Make time to talk about how you are doing. Ask your wife if you are meeting her emotional needs. Be honest with your wife if she is not meeting your sexual needs. (In talking with others, I have found that these things usually work this way round – but it is totally possible that it could be the other way round.)

Take responsibility for your love life. As part of this commitment Deb and I have agreed that we will read a book a year on marriage. To begin with, we would recommend *The 5 Sex Needs of Men and Women* by Gary and Barbara Rosberg. We have also read *For Women Only* and *For Men Only* by Shaunti and Jeff Feldhahn and found these companion books really helpful. I've been married for twenty years, and what I read there gave me new insight into my beautiful, creative wife. We discuss together what we each read – it gives us the chance to look at things from a point of view that we would not necessarily have got to on our own.

Invest time in your marriage. Don't allow ministry opportunities to take vital time away from your wife and family. Prioritize them when planning your diary. With the ability of ministry to take up all available time (and more), putting time with your wife and family into the diary well ahead – and *protecting* that time – is the only way this is going to happen.

Remember the biblical principle of example. Whether we like it or not, we provide a role model for those we serve. I call this the 'goldfish bowl' of ministry: people are always going to be looking at you. Although this can be hard at times, we must not dodge the biblical exhortation for leaders to be an example to others. What you model in your marriage will be seen by those in your church; the strength of *your* marriage will have a direct impact on the strength of the mar-

> What you model in your marriage will be seen by those in your church; the strength of *your* marriage will have a direct impact on the strength of the marriages in *your* church.

riages in your church. This is challenging, but true.

Teach regularly on the subject of marriage. It is important that those in our churches know that our marriages are to be valued, worked at, invested in – and not taken for granted. In teaching on this topic you will refocus the attention of those who are married onto their own relationship, and at the same time you will lay part of the foundation for the next generation's marriages. Those yet to launch into marriage need to be prepared, and those who are stumbling need to be encouraged and redirected. Teaching will be part of that process.

The most important relationship is always that of husband and wife. If your marriage is not strong enough, if it's not overall a positive thing which refreshes and refuels you both, then you will struggle even more in Christian ministry. Even if you have a strong marriage there will be struggles.

Like the following (and I will caricature somewhat to make my point) . . . I want you to imagine a husband coming home from work. The guy comes in – he's exhausted. His wife wants to connect emotionally, talk about the day . . . The husband has no emotional capacity to connect in this way. But because of the way he's wired he still wants sex, because for him that is emotional connection – it's not just a physical thing. A godly wife wants to respond, but it's a lot easier for her to do this once she's connected emotionally. In a poor marriage situation you can quickly get a downward spiral. The guy, wasted with ministry or work, can't connect with romance and giving time and affection to his wife and just listening, while the wife struggles to respond physically because she's not having her emotional needs met.

In a piece of research done on the topic of meeting each other's needs, men were asked 'How much time does your wife want to speak to you in a week?' Their response was, 'Fifteen minutes, twice a week.' Are you ready for the next bit? They then asked the wives – 'How much time do you want to speak with your husband?' Guess what their response was? 'One and a half hours – per day.'

2000–2005:

Three Hundred to Five Hundred

12

Moving In, Moving On

In the middle of 2000 we moved into the newly redesigned and extended building. Five years after arriving to lead the church, we had been able to see the total transformation of the church building. Now, with a new facility, we could press on towards our vision of building a church of a thousand members.

However, it was still early days. In the first year growth continued at a consistent rate of 10 per cent – nothing spectacular, but we were now seeing more than three hundred people, including children, attending regularly on a Sunday.

At our opening evening we invited the mayor of Lewisham to be one of our guests. This was the first time I was to meet David Sullivan. He was generally impressed with the new building, his first question being, 'Where did you get the money from, the Lottery?' He was amazed when I told him that our people at King's had given to pay for the new facility.

> 'Where did you get the money from, the Lottery?'

A number of months later, he called my office and offered to take me out to lunch, not something that happens every day in my line of work. I was chauffeur-driven to a nice Italian restaurant in Beckenham – also not my usual experience! We discussed many things. At one point he asked me how he could engage with Christians and what motivated Christians to vote, and while not really satisfying his questions I took the opportunity to share my faith. I told him my testimony and expressed my conviction that the only way to God is in and through Jesus Christ. A decade later, following a sermon I preached on the supremacy of Christ, he came up to me on a Sunday morning to say that the morning message had reminded him of the conversation we had had at our meal all those years before.

> A 'High Sunday' . . . is a 'growth engine' aimed at creating momentum.

Little did I know at that first meeting with him that ten years later he would regularly attend our church and be pivotal in helping us to acquire a building four times the size of the building we had just completed. Further, he would become a friend and one who would intervene in the life of the church at a key moment in the future.

High Sundays

One of the key growth strategies that we have employed at King's is something we call a 'High Sunday'. It is a 'growth engine' aimed at creating momentum. The new building enabled us to pursue this effective strategy.

Our strategy is simply to build to a particular Sunday when we will pray and invite as many people as possible to attend, trusting that God will meet with them – and that they will experience God. We then provide them with a 'next step' to connect with God and with us. This could be through the Alpha course.

We have run this system or strategy for the last decade or so, and when I first arrived at King's we would probably only do a few of these Sundays a year, or more likely, one or two a term. I remember that when Terry Virgo came to speak back in 1996, which was an encouragement to gather not only the whole church but visitors as well, 205 attended.

> **Examples of High Sundays would be Christmas, Easter, Mothering Sunday, baby thanksgivings/parent dedications, a baptism, a guest speaker, a themed issue or a healing service.**

Simply put, examples of High Sundays would be Christmas, Easter, Mothering Sunday, baby thanksgivings/parent dedications, a baptism, a guest speaker, a themed issue or a healing service. Actually, now we would run something which we would describe as a High Sunday probably every other week. It is an event which will attract more people.

We have also learned to integrate our High Sunday strategy with our overall programming in the life of the church. Our analysis shows that there are more visitors and people looking to join King's in January and in

September each year. Therefore, we now normally plan to have four high Sundays in a row in those months – Vision Sunday, baptisms, an invited guest speaker and dedications. All these Sundays would lead to and be integrated into our midweek programme, which would include a next step into Alpha. In this way we integrate our Sunday programme with our midweek programme.

In January and September we run with a more thematic structure to our preaching – usually a series covering six to eight Sundays, though it could be longer. From February to June we will often work our way through a book of the Bible or a New Testament letter.

We would always put up a strong worship and preaching team in the key growth moments on such Sundays, and I try to ensure that I am in attendance at all these meetings, tending to preach on Sundays more during these periods.

We also found that as the church gets larger it's very important to publicize events well in advance with high-quality literature, and we have now realized that we need to publicize both within the church and externally. We have done this most recently by having an integrated advertising campaign. Billy Graham used to say to his team that whenever he came into a city, if he did not see his picture often enough as he drove in from the airport he would be concerned. So we've taken something of this approach (but my name and pictures of me are not included!) and for the first time invested extra money in a campaign which involved high-quality billboards, ten thousand leaflets, radio adverts and bus stop ads.

13

A Strategic Merger

At the beginning of 2001 a local Newfrontiers church at South Lee, about three miles from Catford, was beginning the search for a new pastor. The church had lost momentum and was meeting in a building which required over a million pounds of repairs and renovation work. Including children, the church averaged around a hundred people attending on a Sunday. As part of my role in overseeing the Newfrontiers churches in London I would meet regularly with Simon Linley, who was one of the elders and was acting leader in the absence of a senior pastor.

On one occasion I suggested to him that we could work more closely together. To my surprise, I had hardly finished my sentence when he proposed that the South Lee church should close down and come and join us at King's. I was open to the idea, but I was also hesitant, as I realized quickly that not everyone at South Lee would be as keen as Simon was on joining with King's – and to be honest I was concerned that such a merger could destabilize all the progress we had achieved in the church at Catford after five years' hard work. With these thoughts in mind, I suggested we take it slowly, speak to our respective leadership teams and, as a small step, arrange to have a meal together. A Chinese meal was arranged for Deb and me with Simon and his wife Sue.

The very next day Annie Twort, a staff member at King's, asked if she could speak to me. She explained that during the Sunday evening prayer meeting four days before, while praying about my role with the Newfrontiers churches in London, she felt God had given her a prophetic picture for me, as follows:

> While everyone was praying together for you I was praying specifically about your role outside King's in the wider London Newfrontiers sphere. In my mind I saw a picture of a densely planted forest – someone was going in amongst the trees, removing a tree here and there to allow more light into the forest as a whole. The forest had been too densely planted – that is, the trees were planted too close to one another for the overall health of all the trees. Some, just a few here and there, needed to be cut down. This brought health and stronger growth to all the other trees.
>
> At the time I wasn't too clear of the interpretation, except that God seemed to be underlining the importance of the work you are doing across London in bringing growth and health to church life.

Annie did not know the interpretation, but I did – immediately. The remarkable relevance and timing of the word made me conclude that God was confirming we should move forward with South Lee, and work positively towards that church joining King's. It was also a great example of the prophetic gift coming at a critical time, confirming this move and directing the church. The application was clear.

I will never forget the evening when the news was shared with the church at South Lee and then the subsequent meeting, giving further details. While trying to follow God's directing, not everyone was as keen on this development as the majority. People say strange things in such highly charged moments, the best or worst at that moment (depending on your perspective) being that King's was only doing this to acquire more money, to clear our £1 million debt. By this time we didn't have a £1 million debt, but this was a moment to stay calm rather than become defensive. It's a huge thing for people to close their church, and it was important that people were able to express their concerns, as well as for the many who believed this was the right decision for the church to be able to grow in conviction that this was the way to go.

Of the one hundred people who attended South Lee at that time, more than seventy subsequently joined us at King's. I estimate that twenty others joined other local churches and ten took the opportunity to move away from the area. That was the only year since January 1996 that King's did not grow (discounting the seventy established Christians from Lee). It took a great deal of time and energy from both parts of the new church to help the South Lee members to integrate into King's – but it was vital to do this well to ensure that issues had been properly covered and prevent such things from blighting progress in future years.

Many of these dear people are now core players in the King's story, and many have become friends and co-workers for the fulfilment of that original vision of a thousand-member church. Simon Linley is now one of our church trustees. Looking back over the years since that significant meeting, one of the most difficult things I have had to do was to lead the funeral of Simon's dear wife Sue, who died suddenly on holiday in the Grand Canyon in 2008. At the age of 47 she went to be with the Lord, by which time the lives of the Linleys had become irrevocably intertwined with ours and those of many others at King's.

It had been six years since I had joined King's. The church had changed radically, was growing once again following a major building project – and now another church had decided to join us. Our third son, Samuel, born at the end of 1999, was growing fast, but all was not well with me. I think I was exhausted with the demands of family life and church leadership, and I approached the elders to ask if I could have a sabbatical. They agreed, but recognizing that South Lee was joining us and that this was a critical time in the process, they suggested I delay the sabbatical for another year. I could see their point and agreed, but reluctantly. Four weeks later I walked into the elders' meeting and informed them that if they didn't approve an immediate sabbatical I would 'go under'. Without hesitation the team agreed – to my relief and delight.

The ride so far had been steady rather than spectacular. King's was averaging just over three hundred people on a Sunday, but the progress made had required and received great effort and application from me. Fortunately for all concerned, I had learned enough self-awareness by this point to read my signals and call a timeout. It was another one of those good decisions! I honestly believe the three months spent resting and reflecting laid the foundation for the next season – and the pace was about to pick up.

Who Cares About New People?

Since arriving at King's, I had been convinced that our future growth was dependent on our ability to reach, attract and keep new people. This may be extremely obvious, but I am continually amazed at how quickly church leaders, many of whom are pastors or teachers, become primarily focused on looking after the existing group of people. If you want to grow a church, the future is in the new people – your task is to get all the existing committed people to see this as their job too. This moves a church from 'Feed me!' to 'Who can I feed?' As Jesus said, 'The Son of Man came to seek and save what was lost' (Luke 19:10).

> If you want to grow a church, the future is in the new people – your task is to get all the existing committed people to see this as their job too.

In the early days of my time at King's, at our weekly staff review meeting we would record all the names of new people. We would identify each one – for example, the lady called Jane in the red jacket. We learned quickly that if a new person comes twice then they are usually very keen to join your church – if you provide a way for them to connect. When a church is small it's possible for leaders to give new attenders a certain amount of individual attention, helping them to feel part of what's going on.

As the church began to grow we found we were unable to track each new person as effectively. We needed to find a process, a way to pastor the new person, and Willow Creek Community Church in Chicago, USA, provided a model that we simply copied. It was there I met Marge Anderson.

Following seven years of ministry at King's I took my first sabbatical, in the course of which Phil Varley and I spent a week at Willow Creek Community Church. We were very keen to meet up with the person responsible for looking after new people at the church, but our first appointment to see Marge Anderson was cancelled because she was unavailable. She was responsible for the integration of new people into a church which, under the leadership of Bill Hybels, had twenty-five thousand attending. We then made a decision I would never regret – we decided not to be deterred but to make a second attempt, and our persistence resulted in success.

The lessons we learned in that hour with Marge Anderson as she explained the connection process have since been implemented at King's – and at many other churches. It was fantastic to find someone so committed to helping new people connect with the local church. It would be true to say that there are now probably hundreds (maybe thousands) of people connected into UK churches because of that hour with that one very significant individual.

We learned the importance of following up each individual who visited the church on a Sunday and how to integrate them into the life of the church. In order to pastor them effectively at this early stage of their contact with King's we set up an Integration Team who met together at the church on a Tuesday evening and who called each person who had left details, making contact and asking about their experience at church the previous Sunday. The Integration Team member would then look out for that person on subsequent Sundays and seek to link them in with others in the church. This process continues to this day and is based on the details provided in the 'Like To Know More' forms which visitors and enquirers are encouraged to complete each Sunday.

Research shows that if a first-time visitor to your church gives you their contact information and is followed up within twenty-four hours, they are 86 per cent more likely to return. Leave any contact until the end of the week and that percentage drops to less than 25 per cent.

> Research shows that if a first-time visitor to your church gives you their contact information and is followed up within twenty-four hours, they are 86 per cent more likely to return. Leave any contact until the end of the week and that percentage drops to less than 25 per cent.

We learned much from that visit which has helped us to connect new people to King's. We have discovered that people fall into a number of different categories. Unbelievers, whom we direct to *Alpha*; Christians who are generally looking for help, who may be hurting and need *pastoral care*; people looking to connect through *serving*, and lastly those looking to connect relationally through a *small group* or community life.

We can spend hours of time and thousands of pounds on mission activities or just pulling off a great Sunday, and not have a way of pastoring the new person into the church.

The model we discovered at Willow Creek was that a phone call and some tracking of the new person increased our connection rate by 100 per cent. Before we started to provide a way of connecting people we would keep about 25 per cent of the new people who showed interest in King's, but since we started phoning and following up more intentionally this has increased to about 50 per cent.

One of the greatest leadership challenges is to predict the future, and the best way to predict the future is to look at past trends. A church that hasn't grown in the last five years is unlikely to double in size in the next five without major re-engineering or other significant change. At King's we have always planned for and prayed for an annual increase of 10 per cent – net. As I mentioned previously, a church will double its size in seven years if you achieve this goal.

Over the years we have worked out that the leading indicator of growth is the number of 'Like to Know More' forms which are handed in at our Welcome Desk on a

> We can spend hours of time and thousands of pounds on mission activities or just pulling off a great Sunday, and not have a way of pastoring the new person into the church.

> A church that hasn't grown in the last five years is unlikely to double in size in the next five without major re-engineering or other significant change.

Sunday. It's been my practice to pray that five forms a week will be given in by visitors/newcomers from our three Sunday meetings. If we get five a week I now know we are going to have a hundred more people in King's in a year's time. *This is incredibly helpful information*. From this we can then project numerical growth, which also shapes all our financial planning. We have a five-year budget projection which helps to shape our staffing needs and our building requirements. All from new 'Like To Know More' forms.

Of course some people leave us; sometimes that's a weekly event as well. Mostly they go for good reasons – but from this analysis I am confident that we are continuing to grow and that we will have over a hundred more people attending in a year's time.

When I leave King's at the end of each Sunday, I am given a report containing the numbers in attendance at each meeting as compared to last year, and the number of 'Like To Know More' forms given in at the Welcome Desk. From this information I can continue to tell King's is growing – and how fast.

Bill Tenny-Brittian is a church leader who is often called in to help churches in the USA that are stuck, plateaued and declining. From his experience he maintains that the failure of a church to grow arises from one of six issues:

- unresolved conflict, which he identifies as the most heinous church growth killer: nothing will change if this isn't dealt with
- ineffective attendance tracking
- failure to follow up visitors
- inhospitable buildings
- unwelcoming people
- absence of intentional assimilation and discipleship
- 'worship services that aren't worth shouting about' – this is the major growth suffocator.

(www.billtennybrittian.com/archives/288: 'The Top Five Reasons Churches Don't Grow')

Leaders! We can be so familiar with the church we attend that we forget how uncomfortable it can feel walking into what is a strange environment, where everyone seems to know everyone else and understands all the unstated rules and protocols. Church can just seem downright bizarre to the unchurched person.

We need to be aware of the impression that we give to visitors and make things as easy as possible for them to step in past the newness and possible strangeness of our gatherings to find out the good news of the gospel. Such an examination will need to cover all we do – and how we do it.

Leaders! We can be so familiar with the church we attend that we forget how uncomfortable it can feel walking into what is a strange environment.

15

A Personal Lesson

It was also during my sabbatical that I felt God speak to me in a very personal way. I was walking in the park, praying as I went, and felt God speak to me, telling me to write down my thoughts. I was recalling what had passed in the years previously, and this is what I wrote:

July 2002

Ten years ago I was 29 years old and had been married to my beautiful Deb for three years. Ben, our first son, was ten days old. We lived in Bedford, I was a youth pastor at Brickhill Church and I had recently been to the States to visit John Wimber's church in Anaheim near Los Angeles.

Today I am 39 years old, happier than ever with my Deb, now married for thirteen years. Ben is 10 years old and I am the proud father of two other excellent sons, Joshua aged 7 and Sam two and a half. We live in Catford, London. I have the privilege of leading a flourishing church called King's Church. I am responsible for the care and oversight of twenty Newfrontiers churches in London. We have a shared vision for fifty churches and ten thousand people in the capital. I am on sabbatical and I visit Chicago and Willow Creek Community Church in ten days' time.

As I prayed today I felt God prompt me to write this – in view of his goodness, and to write down what I believed God is calling me to do in the next ten years of my life. History will be my judge.

- To love my Deb more deeply and be a husband she can be proud of.
- To raise my boys as fine young men in Christ. In ten years Ben will be 20, Josh 17 and Sam 12. My prayer is that I will have fathered them well and that each one will be following Jesus Christ, passionately fulfilling the rich potential each of them has. Help me, Lord – for they are the joy of my heart. I write this with tears.
- To play my part in leading King's towards becoming a thousand-member church.

Lord, only you know what is before me: help me to be faithful to your call on my life. As I get older I am more aware of what I do not know: help me in my weakness to serve you.

To God be the glory
Steve

I remember my surprise to this day: as I wrote down the comments about my boys the tears just rolled down my cheeks. It was a timely reminder that it is possible to build a great church at the expense of your wife and children – I did not want this to be the case with me.

One of the strange impacts of the break upon me was a growing inner confidence that God had indeed called me to lead. Since I'm not known for my lack of confidence, this development was something of a surprise! I felt that God had refreshed my personal conviction about what I and King's were doing – and that it came out of my relationship with him, not from following a formula learned from the experience of others.

> Too many leaders become caught up with overseeing a busy church and run ahead, failing to continue to encounter the living God.

That personal look back over the previous ten years, combined with the 'God moment' that came with it, moved me on in my sense of call to the task we were committed to and also in my leadership of the church. Too many leaders become caught up with overseeing a busy church and run ahead, failing to continue to encounter the living God. This experience of meeting with God reinforced in me the value and importance of my family as opposed to my ministry. I believe that such an encounter with God is a regular necessity if we are not to be derailed from God's purpose for us. Times of reflection and clear-eyed self-assessment are always valuable, never a waste of time and effort.

16

Aiming for Goals!

One of my reflections on that 'time out' during my sabbatical was that our vision to become a thousand-member church had served us well in motivating the church to take on a major building project and that our short-term goals helped build trust, but now we needed something to reach for, something which articulated some more mid-term goals. The idea crystallized as I read Bill Hybels' book *Courageous Leadership*, when I read about what he calls 'Big Hairy Audacious Goals'.

Refreshed from the break, I returned in September 2002 ready to lead into the next season. I met with the leadership team when I returned to King's; we discussed together and prayed hard and as a result presented to the church four five-year goals. Once again, we used the principle of building out of past trends. Our goals for 2003 were:

- to set up a supported housing unit for at least twelve to fourteen disadvantaged and homeless people, and facilitate employment opportunities
- to grow to an average of five hundred people attending on Sunday

- to establish a church plant of seventy-five people in the south-central area of London
- to see 100 per cent of our members participating in community life

While these goals were challenging, they were all attainable, although the last one reflected our value that each member of King's should be part of a small group/house group and be serving in some way in a ministry within the church. It was part of a promotion of the small group/home group ministry and sent the message that no one was excluded from their part in that goal.

Our small group ministry is a core element in the life of King's, and groups meet two or three times a month. As the church has grown larger, it is vital for the life of the fellowship and the well-being of the people within it that our groups should thrive. A number of good one-to-one relationships (probably a minimum of six) are essential

> A number of good one-to-one relationships (probably a minimum of six) are essential for any individual to feel 'rooted' in a large church.

for any individual to feel 'rooted' in a large church, and the small group is where such relationships are likely to be fostered. But the human relational element isn't the key for our groups.

The mission statement for King's small group ministry is: *'Building communities of people with Jesus to change lives.'* The vision: that each person would connect with God, with one another in their group – and with others. Getting to know Jesus and making him known is the primary focus, with worship, prayer and Bible study taking place. Opportunities to share personal needs and openness to welcoming outsiders to the group are both integral to a King's small group.

Some key terms used within the team overseeing small groups would be:

- Accountability: the intentional pursuit of open and honest relationships where there is mutual support and challenge to produce Christlikeness.
- Community: the development of relationships and friendships, with God at the centre, which provide the context for growing in God, serving others and reaching out to unbelievers.
- Discipleship: obediently following Jesus' example, often done in community.
- One-anothering: mutual care, prayer and support which is voluntary and unsolicited. This is modelled and facilitated by leaders but is ultimately carried out by everyone.
- Leadership: the success of a group is dependent on a leader who co-operates with God, casts vision, models it and leads the members accordingly. Regular training is provided by the Small Group Team.
- Mission: we exist for more than just ourselves – being outward-looking is essential.

Small groups can consolidate healthy growth in a growing church. We encourage everyone to participate in such a group – for their own spiritual health and well-being.

It is interesting that following the challenge that we had previously met (when we were at around the two

The next challenge came between an attendance of three hundred and four hundred. The danger for a church at this size is to get caught between the benefits of being a small church and the advantages of becoming a larger one.

hundred mark), as described earlier, the next challenge came between an attendance of three hundred and four hundred. The danger for a church at this size is to get caught between the benefits of being a small church and the advantages of becoming a larger one. It can be too big to benefit from the advantages of everyone knowing everyone, but not big enough to provide the wider programme base and specialist ministries. However, I would reflect that once through the four hundred barrier, in many ways it seemed easy to get to eight hundred.

The benefits of being a smaller church (under two hundred in size) have been catalogued by Tim Keller (see 'Leadership and Church Size Dynamics,' 2006, at www.redeemercitytocity.com). A renowned US Bible teacher, he has also given considerable time to looking at issues of church growth and size. His analysis would be that a small church operates with certain characteristics. There is a strong expectation that every member will know every other one. Informal leadership practice remains strong, and there will be a group of church members who – whether they have a role in the church or not – are opinion leaders. Their approval for anything new will be essential for the take-up by the rest of the church. Communication still tends to be by 'jungle telegraph' – it's informal and fast. The pastor's main role is that of shepherd – how effectively he performs this role will affect how the people hear and receive his preaching. Every member needs to be covered in his personal shepherding, but at the same time growth will bring a need for him to operate more in an administrative capacity. Changes, and the decisions around them, take longer to make at this size – and require one of the lay influencers to be an early adopter and advocate to ensure a successful journey in the church.

When Keller looks at larger churches (those between two hundred and 450 in attendance) he notes that there is a significant change for the individual member. In a church of this size, the primary unit of belonging is a particular group within the church – a ministry team or small group. These are usually between ten and forty people in size and give all the benefits previously known in a smaller church. Leadership becomes more complex as different groups and their needs have to be represented to the whole church (youth, elderly, young families). There's now too much work for only one leadership group or team – departmental arrangements now come into play. As a result of this, leadership becomes more a matter of ability and gifting in those areas rather than longevity of service and strong personality. Rather than just overseeing/supporting the pastor in his role, the other leaders now find that they become directly involved in areas of ministry themselves, partnering staff. At this point the pastor has to become a trainer of others and arranger of ministries. Change now happens through teams who cover particular ministry areas and who have a high degree of ownership in that area. Their enthusiasm and commitment often carries the day in initiating change. I found this analysis helpful in recognizing influential factors in the development of church life as we grew.

Another source of useful information came from a booklet entitled *Leadership, Vision and Growing Churches* – a study of 1,100 congregations, sponsored by the Salvation Army. From this small volume I learned, among other things:

- that in a situation where the church leader is in his early forties or early sixties the church is more likely to grow
- that growth was more likely after the leader has been in post from seven to nine years, followed by ten to thirteen years
- that of the gifts a church leader may have, the one characteristic (out of eight types) that distinguished fast-growing churches was that their leader was a 'Shaper' (this is from the Belbin typography)
- that beyond the leader himself, churches that had run an Alpha course were twice as likely to have a vision for the future as those that had not (31 per cent to 17 per cent)

As King's Church continued to grow, it became increasingly important to have corporate goals which helped our growing range of ministries to stay on track and reminded us that each ministry area is serving the greater good of the whole.

17

An Extension and More . . .

Following that productive trip to the USA, I felt we were beginning to grasp the challenges of church growth, but very soon we faced our next building challenge. Our Sunday meetings were increasingly full, extra space was needed, but how to achieve this? The question we faced was this: should we go to multiple Sunday meetings or extend our building to allow room for two hundred more seats?

Before any decision around big 'directional' calls is made at King's, more than twenty individuals will have been consulted and involved in discussion of various kinds. Trustees and elders, staff members and relevant professionals would be included on that list. It is important to hold the ten-sion between giving a strong lead on issues and consulting widely. At key moments in the life of the church this is an important practice. Proverbs 15:22 states it well: 'Plans fail for lack of counsel, but with many advisers they succeed.'

> It is important to hold the tension between giving a strong lead on issues and consulting widely.

Further, if you were to sit in one of our meetings where such strategic issues were being talked through, you would find the discussion . . . robust! One young church leader from outside King's who did so was surprised at the passion and the strength of opinion in the room.

Following discussion with those key individuals, the next important group would be what we call our 'extended leaders', whom I call together regularly, sharing our latest thinking and gaining their feedback. From there we go to the whole church. Both these steps hone our decision-making, and through them we gain increased ownership for decisions and developments.

In the end we decided that before we went to a second Sunday meeting we would like to be closer to five hundred attending on a Sunday rather than 350. This was ultimately a £600,000 decision, but too many churches move to multiple meetings too early, stalling momentum rather than creating it. The extra demands that multiple meetings place on staff members and committed volunteers need to be recognized when making such a decision.

> Too many churches move to multiple meetings too early, stalling momentum rather than creating it. The extra demands that multiple meetings place on staff members and committed volunteers need to be recognized when making such a decision.

So, 2003 was dominated by another building project. Who would have thought that four years after our first building project we would be into our next one? The extension (which included an extension to the auditorium and crèche rooms behind) was completed during the summer of 2004. We began another 'church year' in September 2004, and then experienced the most remarkable growth – two hundred people joined us in the space of nine months. The newly extended building was full in nine months. This was a first – we had grown consistently over the last nine years at about 10 per cent, that's twenty to thirty new people each year, but two hundred in nine months is a very different experience. It was a sign of things to come.

Yet another timely visit from our friend Steve Nicholson from Chicago moved us on again. When things move fast it is sometimes difficult to get an accurate perspective on what is happening. We realized we needed to move towards two meetings, but the growth had come so quickly. As we sat in the meeting room at the church with the full pastoral team, it was six weeks to my annual study break and summer holiday and we were planning to launch a second meeting in the following January (2006). Steve Nicholson was in the room, listening to our earnest discussion around all the logistics that came with such a development. After a while I noticed he was smiling broadly. I looked at him and he laughed and said, 'You can't wait until January – you're full now!'

He explained that on the basis of his experience with similar growth spurts in churches it wasn't possible to simply 'manufacture' such growth by providing space for people – but it was certainly possible when such growth was given by God to quench or suppress it by not having enough room to accommodate those who came. Once a meeting room is regularly 80 per cent full, the number of new people coming along week by week will begin to drop off. Regular attenders won't bring friends, family or work colleagues if it's hard to find space for them.

> Once a meeting room is regularly 80 per cent full, the number of new people coming along week by week will begin to drop off. Regular attenders won't bring friends, family or work colleagues if it's hard to find space for them.

Something in the room changed at that point. We had another 'God moment' – a number of people in the room started to cry. Sometimes you are running so fast just to keep up with all that God is doing that you can miss what he has been saying through your circumstances. In that moment there was a clear understanding among us all that God was doing something quite remarkable at King's. Two hundred more people in nine months, with all the consequent impact on our pastoral care system and other ministries – but at the same time we could not stand still. It was time to lead again.

I looked around the room at this great team of people; I knew I was about to ask them once again to step up the pace in order to keep up with God.

I asked Phil Varley, our executive pastor, 'Can we do it for September?' He said 'Yes' and the decision was made. Three months later we launched a second morning meeting on the basis that most people want to go to church on Sunday mornings. A year after celebrating the extension to our building we opened the second meeting.

Once again the triangle diagram came into play – we created more space by extending the *building* to gain another two hundred-plus seats and strengthened the *team*. Raising and releasing the *money* enabled us to do both simultaneously. We saw in the space of nine months almost the same growth as in the previous nine years – which brought us from 350 to five hundred in regular attendance.

18

The Move to Multiple Meetings

We are asked regularly about the lessons we have learned about establishing more than one meeting on a Sunday. Our guiding principles would be as follows:

First, it's very important that multiple meetings are established in a context of some momentum and growth. If your church has not grown for the last ten years, it is unlikely that dividing what you already have into two is going to help you. Going to a second meeting should not be taken lightly – for us it was as important a strategic directional call as our £2 million building project a number of years before.

> **If your church has not grown for the last ten years, it is unlikely that dividing what you already have into two is going to help you.**

Second, it should be done with a conviction that God is speaking, so that you can move ahead with a sense of faith and anticipation that God will help you with the challenges that lie ahead.

Third, the move to multiple meetings reflects the missional motivation which is at the heart of the church's life.

Here are some of the key *numerical principles* that have helped us as we have made this decision:

- We have always worked on the principle that when our auditorium is 80 per cent full – that is people sitting down during the preaching – we are full. At 60 per cent capacity you still 'rattle' in the facility. Eighty per cent feels full.
- It's important to work these figures out on your high-attendance Sundays – if you are regularly hitting 80 per cent of capacity on your 'high' Sundays it's time to extend your building, move to another venue, or go to a second meeting.
- As we moved towards two meetings, we worked on the principle that we didn't want a divide or split of more than a 60/40 percentage ratio – in other words we didn't want three hundred at the first meeting and one hundred at the second. We worked very hard on retaining the integrity of this principle, including changing the time of one meeting at an early stage to move people forward and asking a particular ministry group to move to the other of the two services.

> We have always worked on the principle that when our auditorium is 80 per cent full – that is people sitting down during the preaching – we are full.

- Ideally, you never want to be under 50 per cent full in terms of your auditorium's capacity: one hundred people in a 300-seater venue can rattle somewhat. (Incidentally, seating layout is also important here –

we now regularly monitor how many chairs we make available, and where we put them, reducing or adding as appropriate for the numbers attending each meeting rather than leaving the same number of chairs for the whole of Sunday. It may seem a minor issue, but it makes a difference.)

- Also ideally, attendance should be no less than 170–180 in the smaller of the meetings in order to maintain critical mass (this is based on a Sunday attendance of four hundred or more). This is particularly important in a church context that places a high value on corporate worship. If you have been used to a celebration of four hundred people, the worship experience with a group of less than 170 feels very different.

- We found too that it is easier to move to two morning meetings than straight to an evening meeting – this helps particularly when it comes to volunteers. (This may differ in other contexts, for example, university towns and cities.) The length of our meetings is one hour and thirty minutes, with a thirty-minute 'turn-round' between the two morning meetings (9.30 and 11.30 a.m.).

> Ideally, you never want to be under 50 per cent full in terms of your auditorium's capacity.

- More preparation needs to be given to Sunday planning during the week. On the Sunday the pastoring of the meeting is extremely important – you have to start and finish on time, notices should be brief (really brief!), preachers must be disciplined and ministry times (where appropriate) included in the ninety minutes. The loss of the luxury of flexibility to run over time is weighed against the benefit of reaching more people for Jesus.

- We preach the same message at each meeting, and we launched our second and third meetings at key growth points in the year – for us, September and January. We have added the extra meetings in September and profiled these changes with massive leaflet drops, advertising our Sundays and encouraging everyone to invite people along. Our third meeting commenced at the end of a week of mission.

One of the questions we are regularly asked is: 'How do you know which meeting people will be going to?' We found a simple questionnaire to be a reliable indicator of which meeting people will attend. Once we have the completed papers and know the totals from that exercise, if necessary we can ask for volunteers to attend an alternative meeting which responses have indicated could be lower in numbers.

One of the greatest challenges you will face in going to a second or third meeting is the *volunteer challenge* – you need to release a lot more ministry to run the Sunday meetings. So, for us to launch an evening meeting requires us to recruit, train and release one hundred more volunteers a month (twenty-five per week). Obviously, where there is children's ministry at both morning meetings, the volunteer challenge is higher. We have found running a 'Ministry Fair' on a Sunday as part of our

The loss of the luxury of flexibility to run over time is weighed against the benefit of reaching more people for Jesus.

launch strategy to be an effective way of connecting people to ministry opportunities created by the extra meeting. Ministry leaders and their teams literally 'set out their stalls' around the back of the auditorium, and potential volunteers are given information about the work done by each group. Some teams are immensely creative in their attempts to recruit. My observation would be that cakes seem to play a large part in the proceedings – but I could be wrong.

> It is our continued experience that as we have provided more options and more space, God has given us more people.

When we moved to two meetings we also had to pastor the *sense of loss* that some of our congregation felt. We did this publicly on Sundays, identifying with people's sense of loss ('I don't see my friends any more') and providing an exhortation to see the costs of the move as worthwhile as we reach many more people with the gospel.

It is our continued experience that as we have provided more options and more space, God has given us more people.

19

The Team Changes

Over a period of time I began to develop a growing conviction that as strong as our team was, with a growing church and my increasing additional responsibility outside my home church, we now required what I called a 'Big Hitter'. While I did not undervalue the excellent gifts and superb contributions of the existing team, I suggested we look for an additional team member to supplement our teaching ministry. It was over a meal with Terry and Wendy Virgo that Mick and Val Taylor were mentioned – at that time Mick was an elder at a ground-breaking church in Bracknell but was ready for a move.

The problem was that we had no money to employ another pastor, and certainly not one whose experience required more than a trainee's salary. I told our elders the news, but in the context of expressing my disappointment that we could not afford to take on further staff members as we were still paying off loans covering the costs of the KC2000 project and the additional extension.

Phil Varley immediately reminded me that we had been looking for someone with the gift mix of a Mick

Taylor – an excellent Bible teacher and experienced pastor – for a number of years, and further that we had never allowed financial considerations alone to limit any step forward. He encouraged me at least to meet him. From all we knew of the Bracknell church, we believed that he would be at home with our philosophy of ministry and fit well into being part of a large church. I agreed to meet up with him and arranged for an informal exploratory meeting during a break in the course of one of the Newfrontiers prayer and fasting times, where leaders meet over two days, three times a year. I went into the meeting ready to explain all the reasons why such a move could not happen. By the end of our time together I was convinced that we should proceed and was ready to change my attitude to the information that was shaping my decision. As elders we went to the church and told them what had happened and requested we raise some additional money – and with some generous help from our friends in Bracknell the deal was done.

It would be my observation that too many leaders set up their leadership teams so that their own abilities appear to be head and shoulders above those of the team they lead. This can give a false impression that they are extremely good leaders. I believe one of the true tests of great leadership is the stature of the men and women around the primary leader. I am surrounded by men and women of great gifting

> **Too many leaders set up their leadership teams so that their own abilities appear to be head and shoulders above those of the team they lead.**

and capacity, each in their own area of expertise far more gifted than I am. I would have it no other way. As I have said before, 'staff your weaknesses' – and this also explains why we have such a large staff team at King's: I have a multiplicity of weaknesses!

Earlier I mentioned the Belbin test and how useful I have found it. Here I need to mention the Myers Briggs personality inventory (see www.myersbriggs.org). This inventory measures naturally occurring preferences in how people see the world and make decisions. It enables them to identify the work and roles in which they will be most comfortable and effective. We have used it to gain further understanding and awareness of those we have appointed to staff positions.

To grow a large church, you need strength in depth. It also requires the team leader to be secure enough to cope with having many gifted people on his team, not to be threatened by their abilities but to recognize his key role in leading, enabling and supporting such a team to achieve their best – for the benefit of the flock and the glory of God. Incidentally, we did not consider it a coincidence that Mick Taylor came on staff just before a period of explosive growth. This would confirm our ongoing experience that whenever we have provided

> To grow a large church, you need strength in depth. It also requires the team leader to be secure enough to cope with having many gifted people on his team, not to be threatened by their abilities but to recognize his key role in leading, enabling and supporting such a team to achieve their best.

space for new people in the church, God has their wider needs at heart and has provided accordingly – in this case, with an additional teaching ministry.

Growth changes everything, including the way that we lead. I have found Larry Osborne's description of the different levels of leadership in terms of 'sports units' very telling. In his book *The Unity Factor* he describes the pastor of a smaller church (up to around 150 attending), where he is the only paid staff member, in terms of a *lone runner*. He has all the responsibility, but also the freedom that goes with that: freedom to organize his time and develop deeper relationships within the church and freedom to choose how to pursue a future.

As a church begins to grow it is likely that a team of some kind begins to develop, with relationships similar to those of *golfing buddies*, usually around four or so. Regular meetings of this small group ensure that relationships tend to be good quality, and the pace of change is often set by those who have the most questions. There is genuine concern and care for each other – it all feels good and is very satisfying, and everyone has to be on board for things to progress. This would apply to churches from a size of two hundred to five hundred.

From a church size of five hundred attending, up to around eight hundred, continued growth means relationships transition to something approximating a *basketball team*, where the task takes priority over the relationships while the game is going on. The emphasis is on working together, mutual trust and sharing the task. There may well be good team spirit, but people are not all necessarily best friends, and even within the team there will be recognized star players – their presence makes a difference. When it comes to team talks, though, everyone hears the same stuff at the same time and everyone knows what everyone else is doing – and is supposed to do. And while each person has a role, most players can play multiple positions.

At the next stage of growth, where the church is now likely to be over eight hundred in size, that won't be the case. The model now is that of the *American football team*, and if change has been unsettling for team members before, it is likely that the changes that this stage of growth requires will be the most demanding. For those who still think they are playing golf or basketball it will be painful. Highly specialized roles are now the order of the day, and few are easily interchangeable. Teamwork is prioritized over individualism – anyone pursuing the latter can be viewed as a 'loose cannon', especially if in doing so they jeopardize the success of the agreed vision and goals. It's impossible at this stage for everyone to know what everyone else is doing – the need to concentrate on your own sub-team and activities and plan ahead leaves little time for looking at other areas in any depth. At this stage some team members will begin to feel that their contribution is no longer significant and that relationships that were once close and vital are less so. It can take major adjustments for the individual to be able to find a new place in such a growing church, and the personal cost can be considerable. Not everyone will be able to make it through the process. It can be hard for a senior leader to realize this and see those who had been closely involved in the earlier stages of growth decide to move away and find another church. It's a very real cost.

20

Church Planting

One of the greatest dangers for a large church is that it can become consumed with its own agenda. The leadership demands and breadth of its programme can make it an increasingly independent entity, able to attract preaching celebrities from around the world and with the financial strength to do so. It can even grow to a point where other churches attend its conferences and the lessons learned are passed on to churches that desire to grow and reach their own communities.

To a degree we have done all of the above, and in themselves such developments are not wrong. However, you can be a large church and be known in your town, you can be a large church and be known in the small Christian world, but building a large church will not necessarily result in reaching a nation. Ultimately it's an issue of *vision* – are you building a church to change a nation, or reach a town or area, or influence the Christian scene?

This is one of the main reasons that 50 per cent of my time is given to serving other churches, including church plants. I have sometimes wondered how much bigger

King's Church would be now if all I had done was to focus on this local church. But I am also convinced that it would not come close to the total gospel impact of planting more churches. In recent years the movement of which King's is a part has planted, on average, twenty new churches a year in the UK. In London our contribution to this has been eight churches in the last eight years, and we are in the process of launching four more in London.

For a large church to be involved in planting another church is costly. It requires releasing some of your best leaders and other committed people with them – as well as giving money. And, of course, for a leader trying to build a big church, it will make that church smaller.

> For a large church to be involved in planting another church is costly. It requires releasing some of your best leaders and other committed people with them.

Large churches experience a continual volunteer challenge – the larger the church, the greater the recruitment needed and the greater the challenge to do so. Because of the size, there is a tendency for everyone to feel less responsible for what's happening and thus find it easier to say 'no' to a recruiter, especially one they don't know very well – if at all. This is exacerbated by two thoughts which figure strongly in the minds of the large group of people before you as you ask for recruits: 'There must be someone here who has more *time* than me to cover this area of ministry,' and 'There must be someone else who is more *skilled* in working in this ministry area.' The result is that people can become passive and simply come along to enjoy the ride.

When it comes to church planting, those involved have no such luxury – if there is a job to be done, the potential candidates are from the same small pool of core-commitment families and friends. Gifting is less important than availability at this point, and committed individuals are required to undertake multiple tasks and roles. It's intensive and demanding.

For all this, I passionately believe that large churches should be involved in planting churches. In our church movement nearly all of the most successful church plants have been headed by leaders who have come from one of our large churches.

> **Research shows that the average life of a church is the same as the biblical equivalent given for humans – three score years and ten: seventy years.**

One last thought to consider. Research shows that the average life of a church is the same as the biblical equivalent given for humans – three score years and ten: seventy years. Leith Anderson has looked at this and states:

> The average life cycle of a church is a top-flattened bell curve:
>
> | | |
> |---|---|
> | Birth stage (growing) | 1–12 years |
> | Plateau stage (stable) | 12–50 years |
> | Decline stage (dying) | 51–70 years |

Although he concedes that this would not describe all churches, Anderson maintains that most congregations of one hundred years plus are not growing. (Leith Anderson, *Leadership that Works*, pp.26–7.)

This is a sobering statistic. It means that the church you are leading or attending at the moment may well grow old and die. The best way to ensure its DNA is continued is for it to give birth to another church. I would ask, let's not build big churches and miss the bigger picture – large churches should provide the base to send out those who will plant churches all over our nation.

In planting a church it's important for a large church to work in partnership with its apostolic oversight. On this occasion I was able, in my dual role of leading King's Church and overseeing the London Team of our group of churches, to ensure that differing agendas were harmonized.

While King's had previously sent leaders and given money – and people – to church plants that had been initiated by others, I was keen for us to be directly involved in planting a church. Most moves of this kind fall or rise on leadership, and so in 2003 I decided King's would become 'hands on' in planting a proposed church into south-central London, not far from us. I had direct involvement and personal investment in this project. We started with a prayer meeting specific to the church plant which would take place every other week. On the first week we had five people, including me, but a year later a midweek small group was established and under the faithful and committed leadership of Chris and Suzanne Marston (now helping to plant a church in Rio de Janeiro, Brazil) the group grew over a couple of years to around twenty-five people. Many of those were from our church, but increasingly others came from the area of south-central London where the church would eventually meet.

Four years later, in February 2007, during a Sunday morning meeting we prayed for and 'sent out' around thirty people to be with Andy Floyd, one of our young leaders from King's, who was to head up the work. The church was packed. It was a momentous moment for us all. These dear friends, many of whom I had got to know during those times of prayer, some of whom had been saved at King's and had begun their spiritual journey with us, were now being sent to start a new church.

There was real excitement among those standing at the front ready to go. Those who were staying at King's Church were totally behind their friends. It was a wonderful morning. But as I began to pray for them I was unable to hold back tears. I am not known for being quick to cry, but I sobbed my way through the next few minutes. Please be assured it was a great moment in the life of King's: I was the only person crying! We were parting with some of our best people and knew that we were unlikely to see them often as each church set its course and got on with its own journey. It was an emotional moment. In the next couple of years the church plant progressed well, but unfortunately following the death of his father from cancer Andy needed a break, and we invited him to rejoin the King's staff team for a period. He is now fit and well, happily married and, following a redirecting of his future, pursuing a new career in law.

To ensure the continued well-being of that church plant it was time for King's to make another costly move. I asked Owen Hylton, one of our elders, and his wife Pauline to go and lead it. With another ten or so of our people they moved across to further strengthen the group. Beacon Church has gone from strength to strength – they have recently relocated from a school hall and now meet in a cinema in the centre of Brixton.

21

A Place for the Poor

The church at King's had always had a heart for the poor – it would be difficult not to, living in this part of south-east London. Walking through Catford on any day, you will be faced with those in various kinds of poverty – it is obvious that financial and social need is a major factor here. I saw clearly that in the first few years of my ministry here we would need to focus on building a healthy church which could then become a competent resource for caring for those who were less well off than we were.

One of our movement's leaders, Simon Pettit, had exhorted us to *'continue to remember the poor'* (Gal. 2:10). With his words ringing in our ears and the biblical encouragement, we had many people within the church who were keen to be involved in such a mercy ministry, but I felt that at that stage we had no one capable of leading such a project. Without such leadership I foresaw that it would be possible for the church to become quickly overwhelmed. This might lead to the need to withdraw services that those in need had come to depend on. I did not want us to be a source of further disappointment for those already in hardship.

The key to successful ministry is leadership. I knew Simon Allen, who was leading the King's Arms project – a social action ministry in Bedford. He had developed an amazing work there. When I heard he was considering the possibility of a move or a new challenge, I approached him and his wife Rebekah and asked them to move to London, join us at King's and launch a King's social action project.

I firmly believe that the best place to recruit pastoral staff is from within the existing 'home' church – the risks are much lower. In fact, while attending a Willow Creek conference in the USA I heard Bill Hybels quote another speaker to the effect that 50 per cent of all such appointments made from outside the church fail. The majority of King's staff appointments have been from within, but on this occasion we needed to look outside for someone who was appropriately equipped and experienced. These are some of the factors I believe need to be taken into consideration when making such an appointment.

When recruiting from outside, I look for a proven track record in ministry. I am also keen to ensure that we are clear on expectations and would advise leaders not to 'over promise' in a desire to encourage someone to join your team. You will regret it from the day they agree to accept. This would include telling them that they will get certain ministry opportunities, or will definitely be made an elder. Ensure there is good chemistry between you and the person joining the team. A good question to ask is: do I like this person? Would I like to spend time outside church life with them?

Simon and Rebekah joined us from another Newfrontiers church, so I knew we would be on similar theological ground. However, King's was a larger church than the one they were leaving, so I talked through with them the impact of church size. Not only do large churches feel very different from small churches as far as the individual worshipper is concerned, but also the impact on a staff team member is important.

Simon's role would be that of a specialist on the team. Other established team members were generalist in their role. While leading the project in Bedford he had also carried other responsibilities in the church – I was not looking for him to do the same at King's. This expectation needed to be clearly articulated to avoid confusion.

A number of years later, we have a thriving social action ministry called The Jericho Road Project, which includes a weekly outreach meeting called The Feast attended by, on average, seventy people. At that meeting we provide a hot meal (complete with a pudding), and replacement clothes and bedding are often available, as is the chance to speak to those who can give advice on a range of relevant topics. In recent years we have moved into the provision of low-support housing, currently with six houses providing twenty-six beds. A number of different support groups have sprung up too, including one dealing with addiction, and there is help in filling in forms for benefit claims and support to help individuals back into work at the right time. And we have seen lives changed as a result. Former street sleepers are now in fixed accommodation and beginning to engage with a world they avoided – and one that generally avoided them. Many of them now sit in church on a Sunday and worship God together as part of the family of God, a valued part of that family.

Dave – one of those who came to Christ through The Feast – now serves within King's, helping with the care and maintenance of the building. When it comes to assembling flat-packed office furniture – Dave is second to none. But when he first came along after a period of being out of work and sleeping rough, he found the large numbers of people difficult to cope with and felt he was in a bottomless pit. He would sit alone in the corner to eat his meal on a Feast evening. For Dave it was at Alpha that Jesus met with him and a change began that has continued since. On the 'Alpha Saturday' he was prayed for – he talks of feeling 'the warmth of the love of Jesus', which brought him to his knees in tears. Over the years his shyness and relative lack of confidence have fallen away: he can now hold his own in a crowd and is a warm, welcoming person around the building. He makes a real contribution to the life of the church that is really appreciated.

God loves the poor and values them. I believe a sign of an authentic work of God will always involve ministry to the disadvantaged. This ministry is demanding, often unrewarding in the short term and expensive, emotionally and financially. We nearly always overspend this ministry's annual budget.

> I believe a sign of an authentic work of God will always involve ministry to the disadvantaged.

But I say again – God loves the poor! As for me, I am continually amazed at Simon's compassion for those who receive from our involvement in social action. His ability is impressive – as is the team of dedicated people he has built who support him. When visiting the ministry, I feel poorly equipped to connect with many of those he serves – but every time I see them smoking or drinking outside our building, I am glad I invited Simon to come. If my part is just to support him and the team and to provide the overall leadership so that such a ministry can flourish, I am content with that. Many broken lives have found healing and encouragement at King's as a result, and I am confident that this will continue and include many more.

2005–2010:

Five Hundred to
a Thousand

22

Diversity Matters

Along with numerical growth, the church has continued to grow in diversity. Catford is part of the London Borough of Lewisham, a borough which has seen a growing number of arrivals from other parts of the world. One of our elders lives in a small street of thirty houses, close to where I live in Catford. Within those thirty houses, all smallish terraced houses and single-occupancy, the following nationalities are represented: Turkish, Indian, Polish, Italian, White British, Chinese, Russian, Cypriot, as well as families from several different African countries and various Caribbean islands. Local shops and businesses reflect this diversity, and so does the church.

This subject deserves a book in its own right, and I'm delighted to recommend *Crossing the Divide*, written on this important topic by my friend and a former fellow elder at King's, Owen Hylton.

Owen joined the staff team in 2001 and quickly became a key player, encouraging and provoking us to grapple with the issues of diversity in church life. In 2008 Owen moved to lead the Newfrontiers church in the Tulse

Hill/West Norwood area of south London, now meeting in Brixton. The importance of the legacy of his work during his time here at King's cannot be overstated.

When I moved to lead King's fifteen years ago I thought that the church was already diverse. Ten to 15 per cent of those attending came from the black community, but everything else about the church was white – the way we did everything and all the leadership. We had around forty 'extended leaders' – that is non-staff ministry and group leaders – which included just two or three black people, predominantly Caribbean, first and second generation.

While we were aware of the issue, in the first few years we had enough to keep our attention elsewhere – including a major building project. It wasn't until we moved back into our new building that the first black African couple arrived, causing great excitement. Today, there is no majority race – we are all minorities.

We are on a massive journey. I may view things differently in three months' time – we think we see things clearly, and then as time goes on and situations open up even more we have to change. We are learning all the time – I'm aware that most UK churches are white but often seeing increased diversity in those attending, so they are keen to learn about this vital issue. If all we do is get excited about diversity, we miss the point. There are radical implications for how we lead our churches.

Let's talk about something really basic first: food. In the early days Deb and I invited an African couple to our house for a meal. We asked if there was anything they didn't eat – they said they ate anything, but when we served strawberries it was clear that the husband had never tasted them before. We all laugh now, but were all embarrassed at the time. We didn't see – food is an issue. When we began Alpha at church and were providing food there, we served white western (bland) food. We were trying to reach out to local people with the gospel and were giving them a hurdle to overcome by providing food they found difficult. I used to sit at an Alpha table in a diverse group and I would be the only one eating the food. 'It's all right – we ate before we came,' they would say. It took me about three Alphas to work that one out.

Then, when we got to know one of the women from the school our boys were attending, she came along to one of our prayer meetings. I was very aware that she came from a different church background – a black-majority church. We were doing our usual prayer meeting (which we thought was liberated), and when I asked her how she was finding the evening, she said, 'I've never attended a white-majority church before.' I was stunned. I thought we were diverse. I wanted to say to her, 'Look, there's a black person, and there's an Asian – and they aren't sitting at the back!' (I'd been to other churches and observed where people sat.) And then the penny dropped: I was looking from a white western perspective.

The drive within us on this issue comes from a biblical conviction. It is based in theology, not just pragmatically driven by a multicultural situation.

Simon Pettit, a Newfrontiers leader who is now with the Lord, spoke some years ago at our Leadership Conference on 'One New Man in Christ'. Multicoloured diversity had been pioneered in the church he led, Jubilee Church, Cape Town. We must take the theology and work it out in our churches, casting a biblical picture. Things have changed at King's over recent years as we have done so.

We looked at the following biblical passages:

'Here there is no Gentile or Jew' (Col. 3:11–12).

'He himself is our peace . . . and has destroyed . . . the dividing wall of hostility' (Eph. 2:14).

In a surface reading of the New Testament there is a race issue as the gospel breaks out and impacts both Jew and Gentile. There are also cross-class and cross-generational issues for us to deal with. These biblical principles cover those issues too. We have the privilege of living in places where we can work it out.

You need to work out in your context the terminology you are comfortable with. The leaders at King's discussed this for hours and decided on the term 'multicultural'. However, later on our journey, we looked for a phrase that better reflected our commitment to building not only a multicultural/multiethnic church, but a cross-generational and cross-class church too. We concluded as elders that the phrase 'a diverse church' encompassed the breadth of our biblical conviction to serve as wide a community as possible.

Avoid being politically correct – we haven't got into quotas. Try to be sensitive but keep humour in the situation. We are aware we have made and are going to make mistakes, unintentionally offending people from time to time. We are grateful that our black community continues to extend grace to us in this as we move forward into new territory.

We believe that people of diversity are joining our churches for the following reasons:

- *Immigration.* We've seen a huge influx, especially from Africa and Eastern Europe. All those who live in a town with an immigrant population will be aware of this. These arrivals often bring to our churches their robust faith and vibrancy.
- *Reaction to a particular leadership style.* Some join us having left churches with an authoritarian leadership style.
- *A desire to integrate.* If you move into a foreign land, your kids go to a new school and you may go to work, so a church that consists entirely of your own culture can be a safe place. But over time, sometimes a gospel-driven challenge comes – 'If I witness to my white neighbour and they get saved, no way would they feel at home in my Nigerian church.' A mother told me that her children had been asking, 'Why do we have black friends *and* white friends and then go to a church where we are all black?' There is a realization that every other area of life is integrated. When they start to look and find a place like King's, it's a halfway house. And those in mixed marriages especially feel they can identify with us.
- *Location.* People often travel miles across London to go to a church/worship centre/teaching ministry of the type they prefer. Then, if kids come along and they can't get to their own church one Sunday, they look

locally, find 'people like me' in our church and say, 'If *they* have made the journey to a church like this, then I can too.'

Of course we get excited, but it's a big thing for them just to attend. Among other things they have come to a different worship style and preaching style. We must remember as we consider this journey we are making that those who come from a completely different background have made a massive, massive move just to come into our churches.

23

A Leadership Challenge

This issue of diversity is honestly the biggest leadership challenge I have ever faced. My difficulty is that I have never been down this path before and have few reference points. As a church-planting movement we know it is easier to put in foundations at the beginning, but now most UK churches are established as white-majority churches with diverse people coming in after the fact. As Bill

> This issue of diversity is honestly the biggest leadership challenge I have ever faced.

Hybels says, we now face 'the re-engineering challenge'. God is blessing the way we do church, but now we have to make changes – and to re-engineer takes longer than to build from new. It brings tension and we have to hold it together. My only reference point from the past has been that of leaders handling renewal and what I would call 'the New Wineskin Challenge'.

Some of us will recall when our churches went through renewal – typically, the Baptist church I attended went through this in the 1970s and 1980s, when services were a traditional 'hymn/prayer sandwich' – our theology was a little bit liberal but getting more Bible-based. In charismatic renewal, churches started to talk about the Holy Spirit. The Holy Spirit started to take us back to Scripture and to new wine in new wineskins.

I was saved at 19, when Christians began looking as though they believed it. I observed that leaders/pastors struggled with renewal – there was a personal challenge, pressure to change, conflict in the congregation: the leaders knew change was needed but didn't know what the new wineskin looked like.

That's how I feel sometimes about diversity – I feel uncertain and unsettled. Not a great place to be when leading a church. Am I getting it right? Am I getting it wrong? Where do I go now? Am I under-reacting or over-reacting? It's unsettling for both leader and congregation. In renewal, it led to conflict and sometimes to a number of people leaving. Some of us were part of that migration to house churches. The churches that made it through were often led by experienced pastors who had been there a long time – they had a strong trust deposit, went slowly and got the pace of change right. They didn't lose the pioneers, nor did they let the conservatives keep things the same.

At King's, as we registered the need to re-engineer the whole church, we looked round the world to find models to help us – to Jubilee Church in Cape Town and to David Anderson's church, Bridgeway Community Church, in Columbia, USA. There are no well-worn paths here . . .

I am a leader – it's my primary gift, and I have learned that I can recognize other leaders very quickly and want to place them in a leadership role. The trouble is, it's a white leader that I recognize. When a black leader walks in, I'm still trying to learn what the reference points are and don't always see it so instinctively. In a cross-cultural situation, one side of me can see it clearly but the other is unsure. It's confusing and can lead to avoidance if we aren't careful. In our church we are always looking for leaders – if we 'see' white leaders faster, being under pressure to recruit can reinforce the bias, with white leaders coming through more rapidly. It's unintentional but it reinforces the problem. The process of recognizing black leaders can take longer, because we can misread the qualities of cross-cultural leaders.

> The process of recognizing black leaders can take longer, because we can misread the qualities of cross-cultural leaders.

Within the Newfrontiers movement we *recognize* leaders – we give space as God raises them up for their gifts to develop and we recognize them. In some African cultures there is a high value on being submissive to authority (a good value!) and not so much on the need to be proactive. So, if we wait for leadership to emerge western-style, we can wait a long time. We can see potential black leaders as passive if we are not fully aware.

There are areas of church life to carefully examine, including that of community. Here we need to have a good laugh at ourselves!

For many in the white community, our home is our castle. I go in with my nuclear family and I close my front door. If you want to do friendship with me you've got to get your diary out. So we email round 'Need to get together: I can do Friday in four weeks' time' . . . 'I can't make that' . . . 'OK, find a day you can make.'

If someone just turns up at my door it can be: 'What are you doing here? I've got things to do today – don't cut across my agenda. I'm busy . . . '

For many in the black community, it's family and friendship – there are aunts and uncles, cousins everywhere and if anyone turns up, everyone is fed. All are welcomed and the whole day rearranged if necessary. You can stay to midnight and beyond, while I, being white, go to bed at 10 p.m. And for 'fellowship', the white community has the 'small group system' at 8 p.m. on Wednesday evening where we 'share together'. Our black members go, 'Huh?' They often prefer a central Bible study at the church led by one of the teachers . . . a massive difference in expectations.

It is important for us to encourage our black community to step in – white leaders sometimes say that black members don't come and are therefore 'not committed'. This can be a major misreading of what's going on.

Worship is another critical area – we need a radical look at this. Our song lists and our style of worship especially need particular examination. Another of the major examples of this at King's has been . . . the choir! I was adamant: we don't do choirs, we are into body ministry, not presentations. Simon Pettit was very helpful to me on this. In the end I decided that we wouldn't call it a choir but 'a singing group' – because we don't do choirs! I realized that I was being picky about terminology when everyone reflected back to me, 'We're having a choir!' So . . . we have a choir now for major events and still have contributions from the body of the church, prophecies etc. But we have a long way to go on this, primarily because as a movement we 'do' white Newfrontiers songs – the Brighton Conference platform is our prime example. Sometimes the only model of anything else would be children's action songs – a small slice of the variety we could reflect.

When it comes to raising money, the white community tends to give by standing order through the bank. The black community is more likely to respond to an inspirational style of exhortation. We have come to realize that our black members are often financing extended family back in their home countries – there are legacy/heritage issues here, and multiple demands are often being made on their finances. This needs to be acknowledged.

Prayer is another major area requiring our focus. Francis is one of our African members – when he prays, God agrees! His exhortations are stirring. He and others with him have brought a different style to our prayer meetings, convincing others of us that we need to loosen up a bit. We may have thought that they would join our church and do it our way, but we now know better. Some time ago Francis and some of our African men asked to meet and pray on Fridays for a half-night of prayer. But we already met on Wednesday at 8 p.m. for prayer. For a

> We have come to realize that our black members are often financing extended family back in their home countries – there are legacy/heritage issues here, and multiple demands are often being made on their finances. This needs to be acknowledged.

while, I was telling people they couldn't pray (a good example of poor leadership!). But the thing I didn't want was one prayer meeting on this day that was black and another at another time that was white. We now see black and white together at our half-nights of prayer.

Life moments are approached differently by the two communities. Baby dedications – I have learned that there is another way to do these things. We are sometimes invited to go round to someone's house on the eighth day after the birth of a baby and take part in a naming ceremony – our filters as to 'how it's done' have had to be changed. Likewise, funerals proceed differently for different communities. In all these things we have had to learn to become more culturally sensitive instead of operating from the basis of a historical reaction in which we are more aware of ourselves and our preferences.

24

Diversity: Be Intentional

The pastoral issues and legacy issues arising from slavery, colonialism and ongoing racism are huge. While in South Africa, I visited Nelson Mandela's cell on Robben Island. Our guide was a young black man who had been in prison on the island and was released after the fall of apartheid. I asked him why he still worked on the island and he told me that on his release he had gone back to his township home, but he was not famous, there was no counselling for him, no one understood what he had gone through, and there was no work. This was the only job available. He was a free man but was living on an island that had been his prison. That was his legacy.

Most white people, including myself, have thought that we now have a level playing field. We have believed that legislation in the 1970s and since has taken away any bias, and may have thought that some people had a chip on their shoulder.

It's not true. It is not a level playing field, and the evidence for this is found in the areas of employment, interaction with the police, educational opportunities, wealth and inheritance. When we touch these areas, we find ourselves dealing with pain and anger.

At this point I'd like to recommend a book: *One Body, One Spirit* by George Yancey. It lists what he sees as the key principles of successful multiracial churches. The USA has greater experience of this, and therefore more models to draw from. Yancey cites seven principles, and I will comment on a few:

1. Inclusive worship
2. Diverse leadership
3. An overarching goal
4. Intentionality
5. Personal skills
6. Location
7. Adaptability

Inclusive worship: We try to ensure that the musicians and singers on the platform reflect the diversity of the congregation which they lead in worship. The style and selection of songs are also important.

Diverse leadership: All the principles are important, but this one serves as a foundation that makes it easier to implement the others. The right people in place will shape the church. A leader needs to have a cross-cultural gift and interpersonal skills. As I travel around to different churches, some of the 'issues' I see are essentially team dynamics

> We try to ensure that the musicians and singers on the platform reflect the diversity of the congregation which they lead in worship.

between white people. If we add in the pain of the cross-cultural legacy we can misread a situation or miss some signals completely.

An overarching goal: There is a goal beyond diversity – for us, the missional vision of growing a thousand-member church predominantly through seeing people saved. We are reconciled to God and then reconciled to one another – this is the biblical picture. If not, then we wouldn't bother to build towards one another. In reaching people and needing to build them together into a family, diversity is the outworking of the gospel.

Intentionality: Here I would commend David Anderson and his church (Bridgeway Community Church, Columbia, USA) for the example they have set. They have shown us that you need to look at who is on your platform on a Sunday (black and white), and who is doing what – worship band, stewarding, etc. – through all the roles of church life: focused inclusivity is important. You may find that there are a lot of white people doing things, and everything in the system is forcing it to stay as it is. Take the time (even in a busy schedule) to look at this area and make changes – *it will pay dividends*.

There are always first steps for leaders to take in dealing with this massive issue. I would suggest that the following are foundational and helpful:

Intentionally build cross-cultural friendships and invest in them. For me, this was initially with Owen, who became one of our elders and a good friend. Few will be aware that Deb and I spent three years getting to know him and Pauline before he joined our full-time staff, building friendship and giving him responsibility. Build with a man of peace – you have to invest time and effort, and there is no shortcut.

Read widely – increase your awareness and your self-awareness. Be informed! David Devenish in the Newfrontiers movement has a wealth of experience in cross-cultural ministry. His well thought out, biblically-based principles in this area have given us the provocation and the encouragement to examine foundations and practice in our churches.

It has been very instructive to read and take on board the content of books such as *Honor and Shame,* by Roland Muller. He identifies three categories of cultures – power/fear-based, law/guilt-based and honour/shame-based. Many western nations have cultures based on guilt, while many African, Asian and South American cultures tend to have fear-based cultures – other African and Asian cultures and those in the Middle East would be shame-based. As he unpacks what is involved in each of these foundational views it becomes clear that the gospel has something to say on each. It is also clear that to effectively communicate with those coming from within each of those cultures requires differing sensitivities and the work of the Holy Spirit.

Avoid stereotypes. Black people who are late/disorganized . . . I know a lot of white people who are late, too. I watch them come into church every Sunday! Time-keeping is often a more important value to a white person than it is to members of the black community. If a black person is late, it may be because they have met someone and stopped to talk – there is a high value on community versus timekeeping. Keep a sense of humour about this, but take care with jokes.

Don't get ahead of the curve. By this I mean that you may want to establish the whole diversity thing in a short time. It can blow up if you open it up too quickly. Know where you are – take it steadily. Wisdom is required. Weigh all you are learning and then apply it in your context.

Gratitude. I want to finish this chapter by thanking God for the pioneers in this area: that's not me, and if you are white, it's probably not you. It's those who have come across cultural divides into our churches and said, 'We'll jump some hurdles; we like some stuff here.' It is time to honour them, but also to dream with them that we can truly build something that is in the heart of God and will honour him and display to the world around that it can be done – a powerful model for the gospel.

25

Goals and Challenges

On the first Sunday in the New Year of 2007, I stood before our people on our Vision Sunday and shared the newly set goals for the next five years. The importance of communicating with the church cannot be over-stressed. It's not only the team who need to know where they are at critical moments and in times of change.

The goals

Reaching people:
In our desire to extend the gospel to more people, our goal is:

- to see 300 people saved
- to increase our average Sunday attendance, including children, from 750 to 1,100
- to increase our membership from 440 to 600
- to see our low support housing project increase from 14 to 26 places

Developing believers:
In our desire to grow in maturity as believers, our goal is:

- to see the number of people serving regularly rise from 400 to 600
- to increase attendance at our monthly prayer meeting from 125 to 250
- to see 1,000 people attend a training course at King's
- to increase the number of people involved in community life from 450 to 700

Resourcing churches:
In our desire to resource the church beyond King's, our goal is:

- to train and send two pastors to lead churches
- to see Newfrontiers grow from 20 to 25 churches in London
- to play our part in seeing Newfrontiers grow from two hundred to 250 churches in the UK

Then at the end of 2007 we entered what I called 'the perplexed season'. First our church administrator – an excellent guy – confirmed that he and his family would be moving to another part of the country. This was due to the special circumstances following the birth of their first child. Then came the news that my friend and fellow elder (and the leader responsible for pastoral care) was ill and would need extended time away from his responsibilities. In a church of this size pastoral care is a huge load and we knew we had an 'Acts 6 moment'. While we had endeavoured to keep the internal leadership structured to deal with all the growth, our continued expansion over the years had finally caught up with us – our infrastructure hadn't adjusted enough to cope with the numbers of people. We were overrun pastorally and administratively.

It was manic. October and November are my busiest times for Newfrontiers and also the time when I speak most at King's. At the same time we were in discussions about relocating to a new site, which we were told would cost us £12 million (we didn't follow this option in the end). In mid-November I was informed that we were £90,000 short in the budget, with only four months to go to the end of our financial year. And then for the first time in ten years our Sunday attendance was lower than it had been in the previous year. By the time we got to the Family Meeting where I announced all these things to the church, it's probably fair to say that the team was under more stress than we had ever known.

From October to Christmas, any spare time I had was consumed in picking up some of the slack created by the loss of a key pastoral staff member – other leaders were also necessarily involved in this. By the time Christmas came I was exhausted, and for the first time since I had begun to lead King's (the only church I've ever led) I didn't know where we were – an uncomfortable

> For the first time since I had begun to lead King's . . . I was so overrun that I lost my bearings, so overwhelmed with the day-to-day things that I could not read the signposts on the journey.

place to be in, and very difficult to lead from such a place. I was so overrun that I lost my bearings, so overwhelmed with the day-to-day things that I could not read the signposts on the journey. But there were still great things going on. We were still seeing people saved every week and we had 1,700 attend our Christmas carol services.

At moments like this the words of Scripture take on a new intensity of meaning and value. 2 Corinthians 4:16–17 says, 'Therefore we do not lose heart. Though outwardly we are wasting away, yet inwardly we are being renewed day by day. For our light and momentary troubles are achieving for us an eternal glory that far outweighs them all.' When hard-pressed, go to God and his word.

Once again, throughout the season I was learning both personal and corporate leadership lessons. First lesson learned: *Eternal truths do not change; circumstances do* – this is foundational. I found an ability through this period to lean into God and his love for me as an individual rather than finding value in the indicators of progress and growth in the church. It pressed me into prayer more. (This is so basic that I am almost embarrassed to mention it.) Grace under pressure. I was going to meetings in the hope that I would be able to coast and just catch my breath – it didn't happen.

One of the team principles I've learned over the years is that it's important that the team members know exactly where the team stands (John Maxwell, *Developing the Leaders Around You*) – and I would also add, where the church stands. On Boxing Day I got up and began to process where we were in a determined way. (I know, how sad is that? Working on Boxing Day!) I had enough space to reflect on what was going on and analyse our situation. As a result, I came up with six major reasons why we were in the position we were. I realized we faced a series of challenges and that each one taken on its own could derail us. Taken together they presented a major challenge to our ability to reach our vision of a thousand-member church. We were in real danger of getting stuck. These challenges were:

- growth
- team
- facilities
- finance
- diversity
- apostolic reach

At the start of 2008 I reminded everyone of our goals – and spelt out those challenges as I saw them.

Our *growth challenge* – could we cope with more people?

Our *team challenge* – could we adjust to new roles as leaders? Could we go through the pain of counting the cost of these changes? Mark Driscoll of Mars Hill Church, Seattle, USA, addressed the Brighton Leadership Conference 'Together on a Mission' in the summer of 2008. He spoke clearly of the need to re-engineer or 'replant' the church every year and maintained that the main reason churches don't grow is that the leaders don't want to change.

We faced a *facilities challenge* – we were running out of office space and didn't have enough rooms for weekday activities or Sunday ministries outside the main meeting, so we were investigating the possibility of relocating.

We faced a *financial challenge* – a £90,000 shortfall in our revenue giving – and were aware that to solve our facilities challenge required major investment: something in the order of millions of pounds in the coming years.

We faced the *diversity challenge* – the race issue. This was an important challenge and continues to be so.

And we faced an *apostolic challenge*. Could we recover from planting a church in south-central London? After sending a number of great people there, could we help with a church plant into Greenwich? Could we also release Mick Taylor further to work on training leaders within the wider Newfrontiers movement?

This was my analysis: any one of these challenges is big enough for a church. Put all six in the mix and we could get stuck, by which I mean stop growing.

26

Growth: Size Matters!

The most difficult realization and the greatest challenge was that the team as it stood – the one I had built – probably could not take us to the next stage in church life. We needed to face facts. Our success had brought us to a point where the team needed to change. The question was: were we able to make the major adjustments necessary, and were we willing to pay the cost of such changes? We looked again at these questions:

1. Where are we?
2. Where are we going?
3. How are we going to get there?
4. How can each of us be meaningfully involved? (Ownership)

At the same time Owen Hylton left us to lead his own church – an outstanding leader and friend who left a large hole in the team. We recognized as a leadership that circumstances had come together to make this the right time for this move for Owen and Pauline and their girls. It was a joy to know that this growing church –

based then in Tulse Hill and now meeting in the heart of Brixton – would be in good hands. Along with him went another group of committed members.

Those of us who remained at King's had to revise our roles and readjust accordingly. This was a painful but necessary process. Many churches never make this transition, living in denial that such adjustments and restructuring are necessary. Sometimes it's the team leader who will not (or is unable to) handle such a transition. The team may avoid the truth of what needs to be done and may even end up blaming everything and everyone else for the ensuing setbacks and problems, rather than looking at themselves.

Simply put, I would say that by the time eight hundred people are attending the church – and often well before that – it is not only the senior leader who becomes a 'leader of leaders' (Tim Keller). The generalist has to become a specialist in one area of church life and at the same time become a leader himself, able to handle a team. So the youth pastor, say, needs to build his own team and major on enabling and training them to be great with the young people, rather than only being great with the youth himself. In essence, each person becomes a specialist leader of leaders.

A number of my team members enjoyed being a 'generalist' with a finger in most, if not all, pies. Others were experts in their own field, but some of them were unable to transition from doing the ministry tasks themselves to leading a team and seeing the work done through others. As leader of this 'band of brothers' I was caught between the impact of necessary changes on these individuals and the needs of a growing church. I wanted to stay friends with my team and help them to manage the change process at the same time.

Tim Keller, whose insights into church life have helped to shape churches such as ours, says:

> The larger the church, the more the ministry staff members must move from being generalists to being specialists. Everyone from the senior pastor on down must focus on certain ministry areas and concentrate on two or three main tasks. The larger the church, the more the senior pastor must specialize in preaching, vision-keeping and vision-casting, and identifying problems before they become disasters. (Article: Tim Keller, 'Leadership and Church Size Dynamics' (2006) redeemercitytocity.com)

The leader who has become comfortable in the role of generalist in his church will not like this necessary 'focusing down' to concentrate on certain specialist areas while leaving others in the team to cover areas of church life and ministry that have previously been seen as his domain. Others will enjoy the specialist role, losing certain aspects of the overall task of ministry which they found more demanding and giving them to others better equipped for those tasks. But at the same time they may not necessarily have the gifts required to become a 'leader of leaders' – the growth of the church and its transition to another size requires new skills of its leadership, at all levels.

Church size makes a major difference. Keller's research leads him to conclude that the difference between a church of one hundred and a church of one thousand may be much greater than any denominational difference, such as that between a Presbyterian church and a Baptist church of the same size.

Keller has much more to say about the importance of church size and has drawn together some general principles which he sees as having significance as a church grows larger:

- Churches become increasingly complex, with multiple services, multiple groups and eventually even multiple congregations. That level of complexity grows disproportionately with increasing size.
- More staff members per capita are needed. Initially a new staff member might be added for every additional 150–200 people; eventually this could rise to one for every 75–100 new attenders.
- Staff and non-staff responsibilities change. Decision making falls to the staff. Basic pastoral ministry (hospital visiting, discipling, general counselling, etc.) is done by lay leaders. Policy is decided by few – ministry is done by many.
- Communication needs to be intentional and systematic – the same information given multiple times, in different forms and in different locations to ensure optimum coverage.
- Newcomers are less visible in a larger church, so assimilation needs also to be systematic and intentional. 'Pathways' need to be identified.
- The larger the church, the harder it is to recruit volunteers.
- Greater levels of planning and organization are required for events – spontaneous, last-minute events don't work!

- Willing but relatively 'ungifted' musicians find they are used less – music is an attraction in its own right and acceptable standards are much higher.
- Larger churches are subject to constant and sudden changes. There are more groups, programmes and events to change, and this rate of change reflects the decision-making ability of smaller numbers of people who do not have to get everyone's agreement to make such changes.
- This alone may cause individual members to decide to leave. Leaders of churches that grow to this extent are more willing to see members who disagree with procedures or philosophy of ministry leave.
- The pastor of a large church is less available for pastoral work and spends more time with staff members and lay leaders, while not neglecting prayer and time with God.
- The senior leader's leadership abilities become more important – vision-casting and strategic design are essential.
- Longevity of stay becomes important for the senior leader, who is the main source of continuity and stability. Rapid staff turnover at a senior level tends to destabilize growth.
- Small groups (home groups) become the basic unit of pastoral care. This is where individuals really get to know others. The more such groups there are per hundred people, the better cared-for the people are – and the faster the church grows.
- Distinctive vision is important to the members of large churches. They put up with change and difficulty in order to get the mission done – so that mission needs to be clear.

These considerations gave me a great deal to think about as I looked at our own situation. For the first time our growth curve had slowed – we were in danger of losing momentum, and although I had regained an under-standing of the challenges we were facing, one further unspoken challenge was facing me.

Maybe the reason for the apparent stalling in our growth wasn't the limitations of the team I had drawn together. Maybe it was me. Was I the reason we had stalled? I had to ask myself some serious questions. Is this – where I am now – the full measure of my ability, of me as a leader? Did I have what was required, had I the grace appointed, to take us to the next stage of church life and growth?

> Is this – where I am now – the full measure of my ability, of me as a leader?

This was quickly followed by another question: 'And how would I cope if this was it – would I find peace?' Have you ever asked yourself that? If this is it, will I be at peace in my soul? And the answer came – 'I don't know!'

I thought of Romans 12:3 – 'For by the grace given me I say to every one of you: Do not think of yourself more highly than you ought, but rather think of yourself with sober judgement, in accordance with the measure of faith God has given you.'

When you are younger, it always seems there are years ahead in which to achieve all you hope for. 'Bring it on!' is the attitude. But actually it's not about me, or you: it's about grace apportioned by God. And I thought: well, we shall find out . . . and that process continues to this day.

In the middle of all this I found another Leadership Lesson. I was doing a coaching session for leaders of larger churches within our network, trying to explain some of the challenges of growth. I drew a triangle on the board, with one side representing 'Team', the second 'Buildings' and the third 'Finance'. I'd always thought that to grow a church from two hundred to five hundred you need to have a team in place, you need facilities that can cope and you need to be able to fund both. If one of them is not there, you're stuck. I realized as I spoke that this was what we were still dealing with at King's. Though we now had eight hundred attending, we needed to solve the same problems.

Next Leadership Lesson: 'You can only run at full stretch for a short time.'

Upping your game requires emotional, spiritual and physical capacity – after a three- or four-month period you need to dial down so that that level of demand doesn't become a lifestyle. More on this later.

And you need to teach into what's going on. So that's why on the first Sunday in January (our Vision Sunday), and conveniently just after my Boxing Day morning revelation, I stood in front of the church and went through all these things.

I had to help my team adjust expectations concerning what we were looking to achieve in the year to come. Once I was clear on what I needed to communicate, it went well at all levels. We called the church to pray – being open with them brought a great response in prayer.

In February 2008 Mark Jeffery, with a wealth of experience in the academic world, joined the staff team as church administrator. His wider family had been active within King's before I arrived, and apart from the professional skills he brought to the task he had a high level of trust and acceptance within the church. This was another timely appointment for us as we faced the challenges of the coming year.

27

A Third Meeting

January and February 2008 came and went – and then something else happened to me, an instinctive thing. I felt it was time to lead and make some decisions. I had a phone conversation with Steve Nicholson and said to him, 'Our numbers are down – do you have any advice?' to which his response was, 'If you sent forty people out a year ago and you are now almost back to where you were numerically, you have done well.' He also reminded me that the forty who went would be more committed than the new folk who were just coming into the church to 'replace' them. This changed my perspective – a useful piece of information that reduced some pressure.

Well, we recovered. Following that chat with Steve Nicholson we got back to an underlying growth curve of 10 per cent in August 2008. From September to Christmas 2007 we had been in crisis mode. In January 2008 we gained some understanding of what was happening and went back to the team/facilities/finance triangle again. March 2008 brought the end of the annual budget process, and leading out from that we made massive adjustments to our team.

We looked at the budget carefully, cut back everything else we could . . . and then decided to invest in five or six new staff members! A pastoral care worker, a new church administrator, a new facilities manager, two more part-time admin staff and another full-time social action worker came in. Looking back now, we realize we were being prepared for another 'Big Push'.

We looked at the budget carefully, cut back everything else we could . . . and then decided to invest in five or six new staff members!

For the *facilities challenge*, we made the decision not to relocate but to extend the crèche rooms. And we decided to launch a third Sunday meeting.

As for the *financial challenge* – in the end we made a £2,000 loss rather than the £90,000 predicted, and we did that by cuts and by going to the church – we had two Sundays where I did a ten- to fifteen-minute exhortation on giving. We had standing order forms available around the auditorium and encouraged people to sign up there and then. This was the first time we had used such an approach and we found that people responded to the situation generously. We realized that we needed to make giving an easy-access thing.

On the *diversity challenge* we taught through David Anderson's book *Gracism*. When David spoke at a diversity conference we held at King's it had a profound effect on us all. Working through his book together on a Sunday helped to ground what we had learned. We also invited Robert Kwami – a Ghanaian pastor who was now in our church – to join the team, initially for a year. He is still with us.

On the *apostolic challenge* we sent some of our members to join the Greenwich church plant, which continues to prosper.

And we stretched even further by going for the third meeting – impelled by the desire to see more people saved. In April 2008 I felt it was time for us to stretch again and proposed to the elders that we should go for a third meeting from that September. I have always placed a high value on consultation with major issues of this kind and expected lively discussion. To say that their response to this proposal was muted would be an honest assessment, and not surprising in view of the year we'd been through. My usual practice was to present a detailed statistical analysis to support any proposals, but the figures were not as convincing as they had been in the period leading up to the launch of our second meeting in 2005. We hit deadlock in the meeting – I was keen to press on, while others were open but not convinced that the extra demands placed on both team members and our willing and committed volunteers were justified at this stage. In the end the meeting turned on a phrase I use very rarely. It goes like this: 'I honestly believe we should go for this. I believe God has told me.'

It is difficult to argue with God; many senior leaders employ this phrase far too readily. My rule about such a phrase is to use it rarely and do all I can to ensure that what I propose actually happens. Otherwise, if I ever feel called to say it again in the future, I will have given my hearers a confidence problem – in me – and it will have lost its power, falling on deafer ears.

On this occasion the decision was based more on the deposit of trust I had built up with my fellow leaders than on any statistical analysis. We launched a third meeting in the September and experienced yet another year of 25 per cent growth. On occasions leadership is more an instinctive thing than something systematically thought out.

We made the decision on that before we knew the full implications of implementing it. I'm glad that I didn't know that a third meeting would require another hundred volunteers a month to run it!

We also moved into another new area – an advertising campaign in our locality with one large (huge) billboard next to Catford station and also posters in bus shelters. We continue to review the effectiveness of this medium.

So, to summarize the Leadership Lessons of this period:

- Remember eternal truths.
- A good team knows exactly where it stands at any given point.
- You need to lead in crisis – and out of it.
- You can't keep running at full pace.
- Know when it's time to stretch again.

28

Another Building

The successful launch of the third meeting had solved our immediate problem with space in the auditorium, providing room for an anticipated two to three years' growth. At the same time office space was now totally 'maxed out', and on any weekday evening different ministries were vying for ancillary room space, some of which was less than amenable.

During one Vision Sunday I expressed again our need for more space or a larger building. With the completion of the last extension we had been informed by the Planning Department that there was no further room for development on the plot. We had used all our available land, our building's footprint was at its maximum, and we knew from the local planning department that we could build no higher. We had looked at a number of potential solutions elsewhere, the latest being a run-down industrial site, valued at £12 million. I was told that a total of over £20 million would be required for the purchase and refurbishment of this particular site, and following a meeting with Lewisham Planning Department change of use from industrial/commercial zoning seemed unlikely.

At the end of the meeting Dave Sullivan, a former mayor of Lewisham whom I mentioned earlier in our story, came up to me and said he would like to help us find a building. About four weeks later we met at a bistro in Forest Hill, and in the course of our discussion I discovered that Dave had been involved in a number of significant property deals. I left there hopeful that Dave might discover something suitable for us.

Six weeks later, on the Monday following the family's return from a week's holiday in France in May 2009, at around lunchtime, the phone rang. This is how the conversation went:

'Hi Steve, it's Dave. Sorry to call you on your day off but I think I've found you a new building.' I responded enthusiastically and with encouragement, but the shock was just about to come. 'The trouble is, I'm going into a meeting about the building this afternoon – and I need to know if you are serious about buying.' I asked how much it would be likely to cost. 'About £3 million,' Dave said. 'Do you want it?'

I tried to explain that I could not commit the church to a £3 million building project over the phone, on my day off, without seeing the property and without talking to the other leaders. Dave came back at me: 'I just need to know you're serious about buying another building.' I said, 'That I can confirm. We need another building. Please represent us in the meeting this afternoon positively.' I considered I had nothing to lose and all to gain. The next day, Dave walked with me round the outside of the building in question.

It seemed a once in a lifetime opportunity. Through Dave, God was showing us the possibility of acquiring a building that was four times the size of our existing site, at some sixty-five thousand square feet. The cost to buy and refurbish, originally quoted at anywhere between £4 million and £5 million, soon increased to over £6 million.

I had never imagined we would be given such an opportunity in London. During the first visit to the site with the staff team, as we stood outside and I looked at the building, the enormity of the task ahead started to dawn on me. I had had enough experience and had been in leadership long enough to appreciate the additional pressure a building project laid on everyone – both leader and people. All the additional work, both within and out-side planning meetings, that would be required to bring this dream into reality. And then there was the challenge of leading and motivating a church to give millions of pounds. While the team was buzzing, chatting excitedly about the potential, I stood silently in the middle of it all. Then I said, 'I'm glad you're all so excited . . . but I know what it's like to lead a church through a large building project.' Nicholas Ferguson, our youth pastor, responded quickly and helpfully: 'You are made for this, Steve!' It was God's word to me – the encouragement I needed.

Opportunities to acquire a sizeable building of this scale in this part of London, with no planning issues attached for change of use – as a language college it came in the same zoning as a church – come along with the fre-quency of blue moons. King's had grown to a size approaching a thousand on a Sunday, I was experienced enough in church leadership at 46 with a huge trust deposit in our church and also still young enough to carry the project through to completion – I estimated it would require at least a ten-year commitment.

All we needed to do was inform the church and gain their ownership and commitment to raise millions of pounds in the context of the most severe financial and economic conditions for decades! The credit crunch was already having an impact – a number of people had lost their jobs, taken salary cuts or seen pay freezes instituted.

The overarching challenge at that point would be acquiring funding. This was to be done in a context of the banks' unwillingness to lend money to anyone. This all said, there then followed one of the shortest elders' meetings in the history of the church. The opportunity being so good, the decision was easily made, but then most decisions are – the hard work is in the delivery.

Once again I turned to our friend and loyal supporter of King's Church, Paul Braithwaite, whose financial skills and practical experience with all matters concerning buildings had been so valuable to the church previously, and asked him to take on the role of project leader. With typical decisiveness (and despite the fact that he and Charlotte were now living in France) Paul accepted this challenge and quickly produced numerous large-scale spreadsheets – for which he is famous – summarizing the financial challenge ahead.

This decision led to the busiest year of my life to this point. Overnight, additional meetings with architects, bank consultants, bankers, lawyers, trustees, the design team, agents and planning consultants came thick and

I broke almost every rule and boundary I have ever set for myself and taught to others, and began working seven-day weeks, even while on holiday.

fast – budget meetings, Church Family meetings, and just the communication process to keep everyone on board, swamped my life. I broke almost every rule and boundary I have ever set for myself and taught to others, and began working seven-day weeks, even while on holiday.

Deb and the boys were remarkably supportive. There are times in life when you just have to 'up your game', and I know myself well enough to know that I can go to another level for a relatively limited period of time, say three to six months. Good leaders generally have something in the bag for the 'Big Push' moment. It could be in the first year of planting a church; here it was for a building project.

> Good leaders generally have something in the bag for the 'Big Push' moment.

The greatest danger in a period like this is that what starts as a short-term push turns into a lifestyle. Ten months later I hit the wall. I started to observe that I was reacting more emotionally in meetings when conflict was involved, and it all came to a head in one particular week which included Deb requesting I stop looking at my emails on my iPhone during lunch on our day off. My excellent PA, Carol, came into my office and reminded me that I had five days' annual leave allocation left, with only three weeks left in which to take them – a shocking state of affairs, as I am known for having my year's allocation of leave booked well in advance. And then there was the 'open and frank' discussion with the eldership team at King's about all I was doing and where I had got to . . . The combination of these events forced me to take stock and rebalance my life into a more sustainable style and pace.

29

Raising Money

Rudi Giuliani – the Mayor of New York during the period of the 9/11 attacks – says in his book *Leadership*, 'By its nature, budgeting requires one to predict the future.' Following King's Church's success in raising £2 million during the KC2000 building project, I had enjoyed numerous meals with church leaders facing their own capital campaigns. As I dined out on the tales of our experience in this area I had confidently communicated to them that you can raise the same amount towards a building project as your revenue giving for three consecutive years. So if your revenue giving is £150,000 a year, you could raise an additional £450,000 over three years. Then following one phone call I was about to discover if this principle would prove true with much higher figures involved.

Uncertainty and instability in the political and financial worlds have drained confidence in the ability of experts in those fields to predict how trends will unfold. At the same time as the financial slump was taking hold in the world economy we were faced with a unique opportunity to acquire another building. But the cost was £3 million – not an insignificant amount in the light of the global situation at the time. Life became even more interesting and exciting when, at the end of one week, I was informed by our agent that the owner believed the building was worth significantly more than we had offered. He requested we increase our offer, and we were advised that this increase would need to be in the region of £500,000.

Just like that – another half a million pounds. And we had the weekend in which to decide. At this point Dave Sullivan asked to see me. The trustees were to meet on Sunday to discuss the offer. On that Friday Dave came to my office. He exhorted and encouraged me to go for the building, and as our meeting drew to an end he made a remarkable offer which is summarized in a letter I received a few days later. It said:

> [I am prepared] . . . to agree a formal contract to the effect that in the event that King's Church exchanges contracts to purchase the above site . . . and subsequently wishes to withdraw from the purchase prior to completion then (my company) shall buy the site and redeem King's Church's deposit and complete the purchase.

This was an amazing offer! After this meeting I called our solicitor for his advice on how to proceed with the legal side of things. He summarized Dave's offer as a 'Get out of jail free' card. Monopoly (and Risk!) has always been a favourite game of mine. I felt as though I were living it.

The trustees gathered during the second of our Sunday morning meetings at the King's building – while the church was worshipping downstairs, I met with the four other trustees. Within the hour the decision was made, and we increased the offer to £3.5 million. Dave Sullivan's generous offer gave the elders and trustees extra confidence to proceed with the purchase.

With the passage of time and the busy nature of church life, it's easy to forget that this was in 2009. The credit crunch was very much a reality and the inability of bona fide, established companies to secure development loans was regularly highlighted in the national press. The future was uncertain: could we raise the money and secure the lending?

We began to approach high street banks, among other financial institutions, regarding borrowing funds. We drew on the professional skills of church members who had worked with us on earlier extension projects, and prepared our business case to a high level. It was really heartening to be told by a director of a certain high street bank that King's was the best-led organization of any they had seen in the previous three years. He confidently presented our case to the credit department of his bank, but even with such a positive recommendation we were turned down. We had cut no corners in preparing the documentation for that meeting – and meanwhile the people of King's were praying that God would give us favour in the financial realm.

> It was really heartening to be told by a director of a certain high street bank that King's was the best-led organization of any they had seen in the previous three years.

I had been concerned that my initial approach to the banks ('Hi, I'm the pastor of a church: please can we borrow £5 million?') might be met with at best teeth-sucking concern and – at worst – incredulous laughter. Although the process of acquiring approval was lengthier than on previous occasions because of the economic climate, we eventually secured the necessary finance and were able to proceed. Another deep breath and 'Thank you, Lord!'

Vision casting by the leadership is not only important for the church. It could be that a leader has to recruit local councillors, politicians, bankers or other financial organizations and their officials and convince them that what the church believes is the way forward. It goes without saying that a good grasp of the realities of your financial situation is essential.

The ability to raise money to fulfil a God-given vision is a critical part of leadership. I learned an important lesson about raising money as a youth pastor many years ago, and that is: money follows vision. At that time I had presented to the church a dream I had of setting up a non-alcoholic bar in Bedford.

> The ability to raise money to fulfil a God-given vision is a critical part of leadership.

The set-up costs for the project would be £9,000. I was amazed when two church members approached me separately, each offering to give £1,000.

This was how God first showed me that *money follows God-given vision*. It is one of the guiding principles we work by at King's – some of the others are as follows:

- Past trends are generally the best indication of future performance – this would be the case with giving, as well as other areas of church life.
- Practical teaching. We have regularly taught the church at King's about good stewardship and handling your money well. Apart from preaching from the platform on this important topic, we do an annual Stewardship Seminar, giving clear and practical advice. Many new believers are coming into our churches with their past financial mistakes casting a dark shadow over them and their families. For their future well-being these issues need addressing. I have taught the 80/10/10 principle for over a decade: live off 80 per cent of your income, give 10 per cent and save 10 per cent. Avoid debt like the plague (with the careful exception of a mortgage). I trust that this teaching 'investment' will have placed many in the church in a good position, despite the current economic issues.

> I have taught the 80/10/10 principle for over a decade: live off 80 per cent of your income, give 10 per cent and save 10 per cent. Avoid debt like the plague.

- Employ high-quality, trained professionals to give advice. Kindly meant, well-intentioned opinion is no substitute.
- Cash flow is extremely important! As with a well-run set of home finances, so with the church. Know where you are financially.
- People want to give but they need to be asked. Don't be embarrassed to make the Big Ask for God's work.
- We forward-project our budgeting for five years. We

live in reality, and the decisions made today need to be affordable in two years' time.

> **Don't be embarrassed to make the Big Ask for God's work.**

- We look at upsides and downsides. What happens if things don't work out as we have planned and prayed? Be prepared. Think through alternatives.
- Our experience shows that a 10 per cent tolerance should be applied to your annual budget. This means that if you have a £250,000 annual budget, it is possible on the basis of past trends that this could vary by £25,000 in any year. (This becomes more of a challenge as the budget approaches a million, because it is more difficult to explain to the church why we are £100,000 over or under in our budgeting.)
- We keep three months' reserves for unforeseen eventualities.
- In all capital campaigns (raising money for building projects), we ask our people to pledge their giving for up to three years. This approach has provided extremely helpful information for use in discussions with banks.

The church responded brilliantly to the challenge. In the ten months up to September 2010 we raised £700,000 – so even with a less than certain economic situation we will be very close to fulfilling our aim to double our revenue giving in the first year.

Now it's September 2010 as I write. I have just returned from my sabbatical and we are faced with a decision regarding the pace of refurbishment for the new facility. I have pored over spreadsheets and had lengthy phone calls and discussions with those able to advise us, and we now face the decision within the next few weeks of how to move ahead with a first phase. Multiple options have been presented to me – with a wide range of costings, the smallest requiring hundreds of thousands of pounds, the largest needing millions. A mere eight weeks after completing the purchase of a building for £3.5 million, here's yet another big leadership call – and all this on my first day back in the office following a three-month sabbatical.

30

Need a Rest?

While the year that had just gone had been extremely demanding and I had stepped over and through all the boundaries by which I normally ran my life, I had done this knowing that I had a three-month sabbatical rapidly approaching – a planned rest from the end of May to the end of August.

I am a nicer person – that would be on all levels, spiritually, physically and emotionally – when I am rested and refreshed. I'm a better husband, dad and pastor and I also make better leadership decisions as a result!

Finding the best way to balance your life will be very different for each person and will depend on your personality, temperament and season of life. I have met those who see rest as a distraction from fulfilling God's purpose for their lives. My attitude is that I attempt to order my life to ensure I obtain appropriate rest so I can then run the entire race well. I am involved in a marathon, not a sprint. Too many pastors fall into moral temptation or suffer emotional breakdown as a result of lack in this important area. My friend Steve Nicholson said to me recently that in his experience emotional breakdown is not normally associated only with over-work, but also with an underlying sense of failure in the life of the leader which is increased when that leader is physically, emotionally and spiritually tired.

As I mentioned earlier, it was during my sabbatical in 2002 that I encountered God (or rather he met me) in an amazing way. I believe that time away provided the foundation for the next season at King's. I have just returned from another three-month sabbatical, and I am confident that the lessons learned and the rest obtained during that time will help King's onto the next level of our progress towards all that God has for us.

> Emotional breakdown is not normally associated only with overwork, but also with an underlying sense of failure in the life of the leader which is increased when that leader is physically, emotionally and spiritually tired.

I believe in the biblical principle of rest. It is God-ordained, as is a Sabbath day of rest in every week. However, trying to persuade leaders to take a break is sometimes extremely difficult. Please do not misunderstand me. I work extremely hard. By the end of particular days I am completely spent. What I am suggesting is that we all need to pull over for a 'pit stop' from time to time. I am bothered by leaders who don't take their full annual leave allowance, and when I do training for younger leaders it is a matter I always address. It's not an issue of the work ethic of Christian workers – we are totally committed to what God has called us, whether it's church planting, building big churches or reaching the nations. It makes sense to do all we can to maximize our effectiveness on all levels – and rest is essential to that.

Those of us in ministry can feel that we need to go one better than guys who work in business or industry. We don't want to be seen as slackers. We fall prey to the 'You only work one day a week' attitude. I have worked in both business and the church and have found that church leadership is hugely demanding and requires appropriate rest.

In recent years I have sat with at least two pastors experiencing burnout – both significantly. It's possible in serving God to get to a point where we feel trapped by our call. This can magnify our sense of responsibility and drive us to overwork – and underperform. Leaders operate in the goldfish bowl of Christian ministry. Work, church and friendship are all integrated, and it is often impossible to tell where one ends and another begins. You can feel 'on duty' all the time and become 'peopled out'. Some of us have greater capacity for handling this and have learned to establish appropriate boundaries – I have seen others who find it too difficult to say no to demands of this kind. In fact it is possible for exhaustion to become a badge of honour.

Daydream with me now. When was the last time you spoke to a lead elder and in response to your question, 'How are you doing?' the reply was, 'I'm remarkably fresh. I feel totally on top of everything. My wife is loved and my children are getting quality

> It is possible for exhaustion to become a badge of honour

time. I have time to enjoy life while the church is prospering.' I don't think there will be many conversations along those lines!

Some people will continue with unhealthy work patterns because they believe that there is a slower day coming. There isn't! *In fact there is more work coming.* And there's a culture of constant change. The next two decades will bring more to do than we have done in the previous fifty years, and I'm suggesting that we will only be able to do it if we rest well.

> Some people will continue with unhealthy work patterns because they believe that there is a slower day coming. There isn't!

Some time ago I listened to a fantastic talk on work and rest by John Ortberg, formerly of Willow Creek Community Church and now leader of Menlo Park Presbyterian Church in California. He talks of people falling into two categories. First he describes the *compliant pleasers* who have a hard time saying no to anything. They want to avoid conflict and keep everyone happy and can easily feel guilty if they don't step up. They are really nice people, but resentment can build in them like molten lava in a volcano. From time to time, as if from nowhere, they explode.

Then there are the *controllers*. Ortberg says that when they hear the word 'No' they hear the word 'Maybe' and the word 'Maybe' translates into 'Yes'. 'No' is a personal challenge to be overcome, and there is a tendency not to respect the boundaries of others. How we are made and where we have come from will influence how we respond in such situations. We need to be aware of what motivates us to work as we do.

- What am I trying to prove?
- Who am I proving it to? Myself? My peers? My parents?
- What's driving me?
- Who am I seeking to impress?
- Who am I comparing myself with?
- How do the expectations of others affect me?
- Have I a competitive spirit?
- Am I at peace with myself and my measure in God?

Honest answers to such questions will begin to reveal what's underneath our attitude to our work.

Rest for our souls is found in God alone and in his presence. If our identity is wrapped up in our work, we will struggle – it is found in his love for us, his acceptance and grace towards us and not in our performance. He says in Exodus 33:14, 'My Presence will go with you, and I will give you rest.'

I love corporate worship. I love the times of prayer and fasting – three times a year we assemble as leaders in our movement of churches – and I love it because I can leave the demands of church and be in God's presence for two days with my mates. *It forces me to dwell in God's presence in a way I don't tend to do elsewhere.* I return to my work refreshed and revitalized.

I strongly believe that home needs to be a place of rest, and marriage needs to be a positive thing that refuels and refreshes both

> If our identity is wrapped up in our work, we will struggle – it is found in his love for us, his acceptance and grace towards us and not in our performance.

partners, otherwise you will struggle in ministry. The importance of the marriage relationship in ministry cannot be overstated, and I have dealt with this important topic elsewhere in this book. There will be struggles even in a strong marriage – don't fail to invest in it.

You need an interest beyond ministry – whatever it is, give time to it. For me it's watching sport. I consider Sky Sports channels a good investment! I also play golf regularly. Friendship, too, is important, but it can be complicated in ministry – you have to be intentional about investing in such friendships. It is unlikely to happen just by itself. Again, make time to see those who fuel you, not those who drain you.

> I strongly believe that home needs to be a place of rest, and marriage needs to be a positive thing that refuels and refreshes both partners, otherwise you will struggle in ministry.

I'm a task-oriented person and so I plan ahead for times of rest – the first things that go into my diary each year are my holidays, my time off and my study breaks. These are essential for my sense of well-being and my ability to stay the course for the long term. I have a week off at Christmas, and then the first week of January is a study break. My study break is very different to my normal routine: I read, prepare, pray – and play 18 holes. At Easter I have the same routine – a week's holiday, a week's study break. I am far more creative as a result of those study breaks, because I have just come off a week's holiday, and it is my view that the leading edge of my church comes out of those times. It makes me more fruitful. Then in the summer I have six weeks out.

Some of you are now asking, 'What happens to your church?' Your church is far more robust than you realize – it can survive without you. If it can't, then you haven't built anything. In fact you have filled the gaps so much that you have left no space for others to come through. Sometimes, by getting out of the way, hearing from God, being refreshed, I find that I see things totally differently after just a week or two. Build and release your team. Allow others to help you. Give away as much as you can.

> Your church is far more robust than you realize – it can survive without you. If it can't, then you haven't built anything. In fact you have filled the gaps so much that you have left no space for others to come through.

I recognize that I have the potential to become a workaholic, driven by the call of God upon my life. I love my work, but I have concluded that I will achieve more by taking appropriate rest at regular intervals. To that end I have made rest a task and have regularly built it into my schedule.

31

Self-leadership: Ordering Your Life

While sabbaticals and longer breaks are helpful, it's important to retain a balance in life – week by week, month by month and year by year. Raising the money for the building project demanded an extra 'push', but I have now reverted to a more sustainable way of living.

Having looked at the importance of the team around me as a leader, and also at the vital role a good marriage plays in enabling a leader, and having dealt with the importance of rest, it seems an appropriate point to talk about some issues of self-leadership.

'Watch your life and doctrine closely. Persevere in them, because if you do, you will save both yourself and your hearers' (1 Tim. 4:16).

I was recently asked to outline how I manage my life and time in view of my growing responsibilities. I hope the following reflections will be helpful.

I recognize three significant areas of responsibility in my life: home, King's Church and my role within the Newfrontiers movement.

- *Home*: includes spending time with Deb, time with the boys, family nights, rest and holidays. I have particular responsibility for the budget.
- *King's*: leading the church, bringing overall vision and direction, preaching responsibilities, planning, preparation, study time, major budgetary decisions and oversight, key staff, emails, communications and blogs, etc.
- *Newfrontiers*: UK team meetings, team leaders, London area team, prayer and fasting, weekends away for planning or where I am speaking, the eleven churches that I oversee and all the teaching that is connected with my involvement with these specific areas.
- Any *spare time* that's left is for friends, golf and taking it easy!

Each of these needs to be prioritized and put in my diary. I have a framework of working – a daily pattern, a weekly pattern, a monthly pattern and an annual pattern. In order to get the big picture, during the three weeks' planning and preparation time I set aside in the summer I would put into my diary an outline for the next twelve months.

When it comes to priorities at home, these would include days off with Deb, family nights and all holidays. If I can see particular pressure points in my diary, I will try to include some rest and recovery time. As I mentioned previously, I always have a study week at the beginning of each term – usually the first week in January and a week in April or May.

Deb and I have talked through a pattern for the week which would include at least two evenings in together – one with the boys for a family night (usually Saturday night at the moment) and Monday evening, which is our night. We also have Monday together during the day.

During my study weeks I look at my responsibilities at King's. Apart from planning for near dates I look at the longer term, up to eighteen months ahead. I also look at my preaching engagements for the coming term. I have recently pulled together a team of researchers to help me with preparing for preaching. They are given the Bible passages and contexts in which I will be preaching for the term ahead, and I hope to receive from them an A4 sheet summary of the passage with key quotes and ideas. So when I sit down in January and look at my preaching programme through to Easter I will have not only the Bible and my own background reading and thoughts, I will also have four or five A4 sheets summarizing the key points as these selected researchers see them. That gives me a good resource from which to work. My aim is to have outlines of all the messages I will preach in that particular term by the end of my study week.

At King's we like to have the topics for our preaching series well in advance – sometimes up to a year ahead. Apart from those already mentioned who support my preaching preparation, I have recently set up a new theological team to provide me with papers at regular intervals. Creation, the Cross and 'the End Times' are topics that have all been included in the Leadership Blog as a result (see www.stibbertleadership.blogspot.com).

As much as possible I try to keep Wednesdays and Thursdays each week for my Newfrontiers responsibilities.

Emails: I have taken Mark Driscoll's idea of delegating the filtering of my emails to Carol, my PA.

Elders: Currently I meet with the elders weekly for two hours and at other occasional times when required. We have two days together once a term, and once a year that time is extended to a four-day retreat in France when we look at the coming two or three years ahead. And on Tuesday mornings I meet with Phil Varley, our executive pastor, who has the responsibility of running King's on a day-to-day basis.

Once I have looked at the year, I put all my prioritized responsibilities into my diary so I know that they will not be neglected. First, home responsibilities, second, all those at King's (all Sundays at King's, all elders' meetings, trustees' meetings, meetings with key staff with husbands/wives) and third, Newfrontiers. This would include coaching days and any teaching and training dates. I list all the churches I am working with and I get some dates that work well for them and for me. Some of these churches I meet with three or four times a year, and others only once – this depends on where they are in terms of issues, how much they need my input and also how much they think I should be involved.

Normally, once all those items are in the diary it's pretty full, and I find it easy to say no to other invitations.

I like to look at my diary from a *monthly* point of view, as I find that the weeks tend to run into one another. It's important to see what's coming up before and after a week, otherwise your diary can lose shape quickly.

Apart from my *yearly* planning in the summer break, I also review my planning in my study weeks in January and April/May.

I recognize that I'm only able to live like this because I have the support of a fantastic team. First, a full-time PA, Carol, who until recently worked just for me but now gives some support to Phil Varley. Then there's the eldership team – particularly Phil Varley, our executive pastor, who leads the team in my absence. And I also have a writer who helps me with the blogs.

I have lots of support – essential for all senior pastors.

32

Seasons of Life

It was May 2010. We were fifteen years into our time at King's. My second sabbatical was about to start, and on the Sunday before it began I preached to the church about this being the 'half-time' period in my ministry. This was a good time for a break, to prepare for the second half and all that it would bring, as well as to write this book. It's possible to become so consumed with the day-to-day demands of church life that we lose perspective on what God is doing with us over a longer timescale and we can fail to recognize that a new season of life may be beginning.

The season of life that you are currently in will shape you. I found an article in *Leadership* journal (Spring 1996) by Jack Hayford of the Church on the Way, Van Nuys, California, very helpful on this subject. He

It's possible to become so consumed with the day-to-day demands of church life that we lose perspective on what God is doing with us over a longer timescale and we can fail to recognize that a new season of life may be beginning.

saw the human journey in terms of full twenty-year seasons.

Between birth and age 20 was the first winter, where 'foundation points of growth were being made in body and mind while we are still beginners in the earthly journey. The evidence of our true soul is being readied to be made.' These are sovereign foundations. You didn't choose your parents and you didn't choose most of your first twenty years, whether they were good, bad or mixed.

Spring follows from ages 20 to 40. In this period things that will eventually grow into fruit begin to develop. This is when many people conclude their formal education, marry, have children and launch their lifetime's work. This is the seed-sowing time of life, which will determine the type of harvest to be garnered in the years to come. That which is learned in these years and all that is done is part of God's training of you. He is more interested in your development than in your fruit, but young men and women want fruit! We want to succeed – but God has a longer-term view. Hayford says:

> I used to think that whoever coined 'Life begins at 40' was whistling in the dark – trying to console himself. But I've recently concluded life's third twenty-year segment [summer] and I can say around the age of 40, there is a distinct turning point in life's unfolding drama. Our firstfruit begins to be harvested. During our forties and fifties, what we have 'been becoming' increasingly reveals itself.
>
> For example, in my forties and fifties, I found that the early years of study in God's word began to return a wealth I hadn't anticipated – a richer grasp of things eternal and a

new depth of preaching. This is only a sample of life's wealth the summer years can bring.

I'm now in my forties, in the season of summer. I'm now the product of all that God has done in me in the previous years, and I trust that 0 to 40 has prepared me for this moment. It's a good reminder to those not in their forties yet not to worry so much about fruit. Any success before this time is a 'wow' bonus – God is preparing you for the season to come. Hayford continues:

> Autumn. As with the natural world, life's harvest begins in summer and climaxes in the fall. Our sixties and seventies can only be described by autumn – the season of magnificent color and splendid holidays. No lovelier season colors our calendar. No happier times are scheduled than those at home with friends and family during [those months].
>
> At 61, I am anything but feeling old. Autumn's joys are just beginning. I am discovering the wisdom and delight of building new relationships.

And you can also get some great late autumn fruit!

This is also the time of major transition in our working life, when paid employment comes to an end. For churches, succession of the leader is a massive issue. A wise leader is thinking about managing succession at this point, knowing when to step back and let the younger generation come through and make their mistakes. Their gift will still be developing, as will their experience. At this point it requires huge strength and wisdom to know when to let go – and to do it.

Lastly, winter again. This is 80-plus:

The final years are winter again; we are moving toward our term as a biological being . . . There is nothing dour or dead about winter, but it concludes the cycle of seasons . . . Life's winter will finally claim my physical frame, but ahead for each of those whose faith is in Christ there is another springtime, the resurrection.

It's good to be mindful of our season in life, as we can have a tendency to get ahead of God and our own development. We need to learn patience and rest in his timing and purposes.

While attending a conference at Willow Creek Community Church I heard Gordon MacDonald speak. He also proposes that we look at life in terms of seasons. In each of the decades of life different questions tend to be asked by those going through them.

- Twenties – Who am I?
- Thirties – How do I balance all this together?
- Forties – There must be something more than this?
- Fifties – Can I hold on?
- Sixties – Am I redundant?
- Seventies – Was it all worth it?

I recognized that I was now in my forties and know that there is a danger of 'settling' between the ages of 40 and 50. I have referred elsewhere to the study by the Salvation Army and the fact that they discovered that churches tend to grow if the minister is in his early forties – or early sixties. Tucked into this information seems to be the tendency for a 'lost' decade in between. This is a dangerous time! When combined with the questions that Gordon MacDonald provides for those in their forties and fifties, the result can be ministry plateau and a tendency to become risk-averse.

Internally, it is possible to feel trapped. It can feel as though there is no opportunity to get off the ministry treadmill, and can make us wonder whether we have the emotional energy for the demands ahead. Such self-awareness can be very uncomfortable. Reading about seasons in ministry helped me to process how I was feeling. I talked with those I trust, including my dad and, of course, Deb. I prayed it through. Then, when the opportunity came to 'go' again – I was ready.

33

The Move to Multi-Site

I heard today that the exchange of contracts and the process making us the legal owners of the 'new' building is now complete. Following months of hard work and delay after delay, I received a call from our solicitor, Paul Martin, confirming that we were now the proud owners of yet another site. Who would ever have thought that fifteen years after our arrival at King's we would be embarking on yet another massive building project, acquiring a facility with sixty-five thousand square feet of space?

The news brought a mixture of excitement and relief, along with an awareness of the scale of what we were taking on together. The last year had been the most demanding so far in ministry, and even the first six weeks of my sabbatical, which I had set aside to start writing this book, had been constantly interrupted with details involving the building. But we had made it through the tortuous process, and a key foundation for the future was now secure. We could move ahead with our plans to become a multi-site church.

As I have said on a number of occasions throughout this book, facilities – both space in the auditorium, space for our children and youth ministries, office space for staff and for midweek activities – have been limiting factors in our growth curve. Whatever measures we have taken to date to resolve the capacity issue have then quickly produced growth. By the end of 2009 we were full again. We were at the limit of our building's footprint with no option to extend, and while a fourth meeting on the Catford site was considered, our research showed that our demographic required greater Sunday morning capacity.

In parallel to the acquisition of the new building in Lee Green, we were approached by another local Newfrontiers church – Downham Way Family Church, a good church with over a hundred people in attendance which had struggled to find consistent primary leadership for the last decade. In a café in Brockley during a discussion with Nigel Mumford, one of their elders who was faithfully continuing to care for the church, the possibility of that church joining King's and linking in with our move to multi-site was raised. Once again I found myself open but hesitant, not unlike our discussion eight years previously with the church at South Lee.

Two important questions required clear answers: is this a good and right thing for King's, and equally importantly, is this a good and right thing for the church at Downham? I was aware that not everyone would be delighted with this news – it required a considerable emotional journey for some long-standing members. We decided to move slowly with discussions around the issues, but news about the possibility broke in another local church, so we had to bring forward the discussion. The exciting conclusion of the process was that the decision was made that Downham will join King's Church and become our third site. As I write we are in full preparation to become a fully fledged multi-site church in the course of the next six months, moving from three meetings on one site to five meetings on three sites.

Why multi-site and not a church plant?

This is a good question and one which needs a good answer. During my sabbatical I had the privilege of shadowing Nicky Gumbel of Holy Trinity Brompton for the day. He took me round his nine meetings on three sites (soon to become four sites) all within cycling distance of each other in West London. Known around the world as the birthplace of the Alpha course, this is an impressive church. It was fun to cycle between the sites in Nicky's wake and to discuss at length with him the reasoning around going multi-site. While totally committed to church planting, Nicky Gumbel has concluded, as I have, that particularly in urban centres, where appropriate property is so rare and so expensive, the multi-site concept provides a large church with the opportunity to continue to grow, and therefore to build a resource base for its wider vision for reaching the nation and those nations beyond our borders.

> Particularly in urban centres, where appropriate property is so rare and so expensive, the multi-site concept provides a large church with the opportunity to continue to grow.

At King's, we are excited at the new opportunities that the multi-site option gives us. At the same time we face the challenge of re-engineering the church leadership team once again. The latest developments mean that we will be scattered across three sites, running at least five meetings and caring for growing numbers in an increasingly diverse community across the divisions of age, ethnic mix and social grouping. As a result, as I write this, I am in the process of discussing the consequences of these new demands with team members and asking some of them to relocate to one of the other sites.

Another important decision to be made soon concerns the speed of the redevelopment of the Downham and Lee Green sites, and the major issue of volunteer recruitment within the church needs to be further grappled with. Apart from relocating staff team members, we will also need some key church members – the backbone of the essential ministries of the church – to consider moving to another site in order to ensure that we can support all that needs to be done in the ministries we provide. This is no small 'ask' – it will stretch our people resources and require some of our core people to prioritize serving in a way that will remove them from regular contact with friends and others with whom they have worked and served, in some cases for years.

While remaining clear-sighted about all that is required at the moment, we need to lift our eyes to the future and look ahead to ensure that current decisions will not compromise long-term plans. Two to five years ahead the consequences of decisions made now will impact the direction to be taken and the speed at which it can be taken – as well as the resources that are available.

For us this means looking at issues such as: how many sites will we have in five years' time? Will it be three – or six? This decision alone brings huge implications – all the reading I have done around this topic indicates that while a team can continue to function as before over three or four sites, any further growth requires major restructuring – again. We also need to decide whether to continue with 'live' preaching in all three sites, or to transition to DVD recordings or a combination of both. Some multi-site churches project the live preaching from one site to the others. Such options involve massive financial investment in people or technology – or most likely, both.

Already we have been placing team members to cover what we see as strategic points. Since the start of 2010 Martin Alley has been devoting his time to the Downham Church. We have had excellent responses from them to his input. In addition, from January 2011 Ben Welchman, who has been on staff since 2003 and who has been youth pastor and small group pastor in turn, will become the site leader at Downham. We consider that the gifts that Ben and Martin bring to this 'ready for growth' situation are a great investment of King's resources.

Also during this year we have had another 'big hitter' join us. Malcolm Kyte, previously lead elder at Queen's Road Church, Wimbledon, has come on staff to head up the rapidly growing pastoral team. When we thought about such an appointment it seemed a big ask to make of Malcolm, an experienced pastor. I was delighted that he was open to consider such a move and even more delighted when he and Cathy agreed to join us. It is not every leader who can come and serve another's vision after he has led his own team and established a successful work elsewhere. Malcolm and Cathy declared themselves ready for a new challenge, and we are very grateful.

While the oversight of all the pastoral work comes within Malcolm's remit, God had previously provided additional pastoral support for our team in the shape of Hilary Dalziel. Hilary and her husband William came to us from Miami, where William's work had located them. Florida to Catford is not an obvious progression – if not for God, would such a thing be possible? During their years in the USA Hilary had undertaken theological and pastoral training and had worked as a hospital chaplain in a huge hospital. When she began to work for King's in 2008 she brought a focus and breadth to our pastoral work enhanced by professional training. This has brought confidence and security to both the elders and the church as a whole.

All this gives us further confidence as we try to deploy our staff team members and adapt our structures for the future. As we look at recent years, we see how God has been bringing into our church and team those who would be able to bear weight and take the work forward. That our pastoral team is now as large and as strong as it is not only reassures us now – it increases our faith for the future.

But there is still much to do. We need to work out how individual site leaders will relate to the elders and other members of the pastoral team who have wider responsibility across the whole church. This is a pressing matter that will have major repercussions and will require review and reassessment.

It has been my practice up to now only to adopt new ideas that have been road-tested well in the UK before integrating them into our own philosophy of ministry. On this issue we feel we are, along with a few other UK churches, at the cutting edge of this approach to church growth – a phenomenon which has exploded in the USA during the last decade but which has few working models on this side of the Atlantic. As a result, where in the rest of the book I have been able to present concepts and practices that have worked within our context, on this subject we are still developing principles and practice and we are having to learn fast. Recognizing that at this stage in this exciting time we have more questions than answers, we still believe that the potential for gospel breakthrough that it presents is well worth the risk. In the future we shall be able to share from our experience – we look forward to that time!

34

A Continuing Story

At the very heart of this book is my conviction that many churches fail to fulfil their full growth potential and as a result reduce their ability to reach people for Jesus. The fundamental reason for this, as I see it, is that the scope of the values that are so precious to us is limited because the role of leadership and the place of 'new wineskins' are undervalued in effectively pastoring an ever-growing group of disciples.

I love the book of Acts. The phrase 'the Lord added daily those being saved' contains within it a great sense of momentum and gospel breakthrough. Acts 6 records the impact of such growth within the fellowship of believers – people began to be overlooked in the pastoral care which involved distribution of food to those who had no other means of support. The Greek-speaking Jews started complaining against the Hebraic Jews, as a result of which the apostles were presented with a growth, class and cultural challenge.

Their response was to prioritize their own roles and release others to care for the ever-increasing community. The outcome of this leadership call is recorded in Acts 6:7:

'So the word of God spread. The number of disciples in Jerusalem increased rapidly, and a large number of priests became obedient to the faith.' The emphasis in Acts 6 is on the gospel impact of this leadership decision rather than on the fact that those who were previously overlooked were now being cared for, important though that was. The change of the leadership 'wineskin' – a major shift in working structure – is driven by the missionary impulse, rather than by pastoral concern alone.

One of the key principles presented in this book has been: *Know yourself, Build a team, Grow a church*. I believe this is at the heart of what the apostles did in response to the growth of the gospel, and our own experience at King's is a lasting testimony to the vital role of team in our growth.

Recently, on one of our regular Vision Sundays, I exhorted the church at King's to 'advance' again. Fifteen years after our arrival to lead a struggling church, we are now positioned for another period of growth and gospel extension. On the basis of our recent trajectory we could well be gathering 1,500 people each Sunday in a few years.

This church that I lead in London has great potential to reach hundreds and even thousands for Christ in the next two decades. I am hoping and praying that the best is still to come. If past performance is the best indicator of future performance, the future is bright, and while we are expectant, it is good to hold things lightly and be humble before God – only he knows what lies ahead for us all.

During my time in ministry I have had the privilege of visiting many and various churches in a wide range of cultures and nations. It is evident, even from such brief visits, that God's church is wonderfully diverse, each church with its own flavour and style. King's certainly reflects my style and flavour of leadership, and the biblical values which are so precious to us. While I hope you have enjoyed and benefited from reading our story, I would ask you to make sure you contextualize it in your own situation. This is not the *only* way to lead a growing church. Further, I would say that we must always remember Paul's exhortation in 1 Corinthians 3:6, 'I planted the seed, Apollos watered it, but God made it grow.'

God involves us in *his* great mission, but we can save no one – Jesus Christ is our Saviour, and while human leadership is critical, those of us who are leaders should not overestimate our importance in the great scheme of things.

> God involves us in *his* great mission, but we can save no one – Jesus Christ is our Saviour, and while human leadership is critical, those of us who are leaders should not overestimate our importance in the great scheme of things.

When I moved to London to lead King's Church, I was convinced that if we were serious about seeing the nation won for Christ then we needed to relocate from a position where we had strong, established provincial churches to one where we were investing, both financially and in human resources, in the major cities of our nation. Such investment is strategic as far as I am concerned, and I know that many others would share my view on this.

At the time when I was considering my own future, I was personally encouraged by prophetic words and pictures from those I respected but who did not, at that time, know the options and the decisions that were being made. One such word picture was from my good friend Mark Landreth-Smith, who gave me the following: 'Sand, sand, sand, pebbles, pebbles, pebbles, pavement, pavement, pavement.'

He was unaware that I had been asked to consider leading two other churches, both on the coast. It was the pavements of London that won my attention – and my heart – and since that time it has been the twin tracks of the strategic and the prophetic that have carried us forward. I would not want it any other way.

The years speed past. Life is busy – but equally, life is short. I know how I want to spend my life, so I don't hesitate to encourage others – and strongly: 'Don't waste it!' Make sure you give your time and energy to that which has lasting, eternal significance. Whether you serve in what you consider to be the background in your church, or carry the huge privilege and the weight of leading God's people, you are about a glorious work.

When everything in history is finished and the old heavens and earth are rolled up and done with, the church will still stand. We are the hope of the world. What greater task could there be than to work with the Master Builder to accomplish his Master Work? To give the best of our abilities and achieve maximum effectiveness is not a matter of our own satisfaction and self-fulfilment – it is crucial for the eternal well-being of so many who live on our doorstep. I hope and trust that what I have shared in these pages might help others to think through how they do what they do.

Meanwhile, at King's we will continue with our task. Who knows what lies ahead? We were unable to foresee the international financial crash and avoid its consequences: it will continue to shape our world for years to come. But while we minister to a broken world and hold out to it the good news, we will never be without a harvest field. God is good and will provide for his work.

As for me – I intend to continue to lead the people God has given me with all my energy and skill. I continue to be deeply grateful to those who have joined me on this marathon and who have stepped up at each stage to ensure that we stay effective in our task. We have run together, and by God's grace we have not run aimlessly or in vain. The aim of running is to get to the finish: I intend to continue to be intentional about running well, resting well and finishing well. My aim is to go through the finishing line at speed – to the glory of God.

Postscript

Sunday 3 April 2011

Today, some four weeks after going 'live' as a multi-site church, we saw 1,400 people gather over our three sites – our largest attendance ever and another first for King's. Nine months after acquiring our new building we moved in and are already seeing amazing signs of early growth. Our preaching team members, having become used to preaching three times, are now beginning the adjustment to speaking five times on a Sunday. We have even tested the contingency plan when the designated preacher (me!) went sick on the Saturday and another team member had to step in with 24 hours' notice! That's what team is for – and I was very grateful at that moment to be part of a gifted and equipped team. The church continues to give generously with over £1 million given to the building project in the last 18 months. And, praise God, King's Church continues to grow in diversity.

Six weeks prior to the launch to multi-site I called the church to 40 days of prayer and fasting. During this time we asked our small groups to set aside their programme so that the whole church could come together each Wednesday evening at the Catford building for prayer and celebration. The response was tremendous! The turnout showed the high level of ownership that the church had for all that was ahead – the worship was superb, there was a hunger for God's Word, and as we prayed there was an amazing sense of God's presence with us. Digging deeper into God at such a time is excellent preparation for all that is ahead, some of which we are aware of and some – well, we shall find out as we go! Those who came to those evenings found these times to be faith-building as we focused on Jesus and knew the Holy Spirit present with us.

Given the number of people gathering on the three sites from the start, we are already considering the possibility of multiple meetings on our two new sites and also whether we will open up further sites in south-east London. These possibilities raise big questions for the future. Meanwhile, everyone at King's Church will continue to adjust to all the demands of this new phase in growing the church, but God is good – and it is *Good to Grow*!

Appendix

King's Church Statements

Mission Statement: why we exist

Building a diverse church serving the communities of south-east London.

Vision Statement: what we intend to do

- *It is a dream of a place where the hurting, the depressed, the frustrated and the confused can find love, acceptance, help, hope, forgiveness, guidance, encouragement and purpose.*
- *It is a dream of sharing the good news of Jesus Christ with thousands of residents in London.*
- *It is a dream of welcoming 1,000 members into fellowship in our church family made up of all generations and many nationalities.*
- *It is a dream of developing people to spiritual maturity, living out a life full of worship to the risen Lord Jesus.*
- *It is a dream of being a training centre which will equip every believer for significant ministry and send many*

across the nation and the nations on short-term and longer-term mission.

- *It is a dream of reproducing ourselves by planting at least one church every five years.*
- *It is a dream of having a facility which can serve our local needs, as well as serving regionally.*

Steve Tibbert, Senior Pastor, September 1997

Values Statement: what we practise

- *We want the grace of God to be characteristic of every aspect of our life as a church. (2 Cor. 1:12; 9:8; Col. 4:6; Titus 2:11)*
- *The Bible is our authoritative guide in all matters of faith and practice. We therefore place great importance on regular teaching from the scriptures when we meet together. (2 Tim. 3:16; Titus 2:1; Col. 3:16; 1 Tim. 4:13)*
- *We see prayer as vital and fundamental to all we do. (Eph. 6:18; Phil. 4:6; 1 Tim. 2:1–2)*
- *When we come together to worship, we seek both the freedom and the order that are given by the Holy Spirit. (John 4:24; 1 Cor. 14:39–40)*
- *We are all called to be active participants in the worship, life and mission of the church, which is Christ's body, God's chosen instrument for the advancement of his Kingdom. (Rom. 12:4–8; Eph. 4:16)*
- *We want to demonstrate the love of God and share the good news about Jesus to people in our society. (Mark 12:31; Luke 9:2; Gal. 6:10; Rom. 1:16)*
- *Those who repent and believe are to be baptized in water as a demonstration of death to sin and new life in Christ. (Matt. 28:19; Rom. 6:2–4)*

- *Baptism in the Spirit and being continually filled with the Spirit gives us close relationship with God and power for discipleship. (Acts 1:5; Eph. 5:18)*
- *As disciples of Christ, we are called to develop our relationship with God and to grow in character and maturity. (Gal. 5:22–26; Eph. 4:13; 2 Tim. 3:14–17)*
- *As a gathering of people who are committed to Jesus and to one another, we want to build godly relationships in our family units, in our small groups and in the wider church setting. (John 13:34–35; Rom. 15:7; Eph. 5:21 – 6:4)*
- *We break bread and drink wine together regularly to remember the death of Jesus and look forward to his return. (1 Cor. 11:23–26)*
- *One way we show our commitment to the church is by giving financially in proportion to our resources. (1 Cor. 16:2; 2 Cor. 9:7)*
- *The ministry of apostles, prophets, evangelists, pastors and teachers, and that of our own leaders, is recognized by us and welcomed among us. (Heb. 13:17; Eph. 4:11–12)*
- *We are only part of the body of Christ and therefore welcome fellowship with all Christians. (Rom. 15:7; 1 Cor. 12:27)*

Faith Statement: what we believe

The Bible

We believe that God inspired the words of the Bible to be written. The Bible is the supreme authority to which we refer in all matters of faith and practice.
(Ps. 119:105; 2 Tim. 3:16; 2 Pet. 1:19–21)

God

We believe in the three-fold revelation of God as Father, Son and Holy Spirit, given in the Old and New Testaments of the Bible. We believe that God is sovereign: in creation, in sustaining the universe, in the revelation of himself, in saving mankind and in the final judgement of all people. He works out everything in accordance with his will.

(Gen. 1:1; Ps. 90:2; Matt. 28:19; 1 Pet. 1:2; Col. 1:15–17)

Jesus

We believe that Jesus Christ is the Son of God. He is both fully God and fully man. He lived a sinless human life and offered himself as the perfect sacrifice for the sins of all mankind by dying on a cross. He rose from the dead and is now at God's right hand, interceding for his people and ruling as Lord over all.

(Col. 2:9; 1 Cor. 15:3–4; Phil. 2:6–11; Rom. 8:34)

The Holy Spirit

We believe that the Holy Spirit is equal with the Father and the Son as God. It is he who makes people aware of their sin and their need of God and he lives in the hearts of all Christians. He reveals spiritual truth to us, gives us power for living and changes us to be more like Jesus.

(Gen. 1:2; 2 Cor. 3:7; John 14:16–17; John 16:8; Acts 1:8)

Mankind

We believe that God made man – male and female – in his own image, as the crown of creation, to have fellowship with him. However, because of sin, we are all guilty before God and subject to his wrath and condemnation.

(Gen. 1:27; Ps. 8:4; Rom. 3:23; Rom. 14:10; Eph. 2:3)

Salvation

We believe that salvation is a gift of God to man. God has had an eternal plan to rescue people from sin, death and hell and to bring them into a relationship with himself which they will enjoy both here on earth and with him in heaven for eternity. We are saved when we turn from our sin and put our trust in the crucified and risen Lord Jesus; this is solely by God's grace, and not because of anything good we have done.
(Rom. 1:17; Eph. 2:8; 1 Thess. 1:10; 2 Tim. 1:9)

The Church

We believe in one universal church, made up of all true followers of Jesus Christ. We believe that all Christians need to be committed to a local church, where they can join with other believers in worshipping God and showing his love to others.
(1 Cor. 1:2; Heb. 10:25; Eph. 2:19–22; Eph. 3:10–11)

The Return of Jesus

We believe in a future, personal, visible return of the Lord Jesus to the earth in power and glory.
(Matt. 16:27; Matt. 26:64; Acts 1:11; Rev. 22:12)

Bibliography

Anderson, David – *Gracism*. Nottingham: IVP, 2007.

Anderson, David and Brent Zuercher – *Letters Across the Divide*. Grand Rapids: Baker, 2001.

Anderson, Leith – *Leadership that Works*. Minneapolis: Bethany, 1999.

Chapman, Gary – *The 5 Love Languages*. Chicago: Northfield, 2004 ed.

Clinton, Dr J. Robert – *The Making of a Leader*. Colorado Springs: NavPress, 1988.

Collins, Jim – *Good to Great*. London: Random House, 2001.

Collins, Jim – *Good to Great in the Social Sectors*. London: Random House, 2006.

Devenish, David – *What on Earth is the Church For?* Milton Keynes: Authentic, 2005.

Driscoll, Mark – *Confessions of a Reformission Rev.* Grand Rapids: Zondervan, 2006.

Evans, Debra – *The Christian Woman's Guide to Sexuality*. Wheaton: Crossway, 1997.

Feldhahn, Shaunti – *For Women Only*. Colorado Springs: Multnomah, 2004.

Feldhahn, Shaunti and Jeff – *For Men Only*. Colorado Springs: Multnomah, 2006.

Giuliani, Rudolph W. – *Leadership*. London: Little, Brown, 2002.

Hayford, Jack – 'Your Season of Ministry', *Leadership* (Spring 1996), p. 45.

Hybels, Bill – *Axiom*. Grand Rapids: Zondervan, 2008.

Hybels, Bill – *Courageous Leadership*. Grand Rapids: Zondervan, 2002.

Hylton, Owen – *Crossing the Divide*. Nottingham: IVP, 2009.

Leman, Dr Kevin – *Sheet Music*. Wheaton: Tyndale, 2003.

Maxwell, John – *The 21 Irrefutable Laws of Leadership*. Nashville: Thomas Nelson, 1998.

Maxwell, John – *Developing the Leaders Around You*. Nashville: Thomas Nelson, 1995.

Maxwell, John – *Developing the Leader Within You*. Nashville: Thomas Nelson, 1993.

Maxwell, John – *The 17 Indisputable Laws of Teamwork*. Nashville: Thomas Nelson, 2001.

Maxwell, John – *The 360⁰ Leader*. Nashville: Thomas Nelson, 2005.

Muller, Roland – *Honor and Shame*. USA: Xlibris Corporation, 2000.

Osborne, Larry W. – *The Unity Factor*. Vista: Owl's Nest, 1989.

Rosberg, Dr Gary and Barbara – *The 5 Sex Needs of Men and Women*. Illinois: Tyndale, 2006.

Schwarz, Christian – *Natural Church Development* (UK edition: trans. and ed. L. McAdam, L. Wollin, M. Wollin, M. Hill, S. Harvey). Bedford: British Church Growth Association, 1996.

Warren, Rick – *The Purpose Driven Church*. Grand Rapids: Zondervan, 1995.

Warren, Robert – *Building Missionary Congregations*. London: Church House, 1995.

Watson, David – *I Believe in Evangelism*. Sevenoaks: Hodder and Stoughton, rev. edn, 1979.

Yancey, George – *One Body, One Spirit*. Downers Grove: IVP, 2003.

Booklet:

Leadership, Vision and Growing Churches – a study sponsored by The Salvation Army, published by Christian Research, 2003 (www.christian-research.org.uk).

Internet:

Keller, Tim – 'Leadership and Church Size Dynamics' www.redeemercitytocity.com, 2006.

Keller, Tim – 'Process-Managing: Church Size' claypeck.com/articles/process-managing-church-size-tim-keller

Tenny-Brittian, Bill – 'The Top Five Reasons Churches Don't Grow': www.billtennybrittian.com/archives/288.

www.belbin.com

www.myersbriggs.org

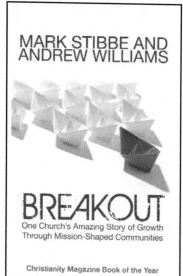

Breakout

One Church's Amazing Story of Growth Through Mission-Shaped Communities

Mark Stibbe and Andrew Williams

978-1-86024-596-1

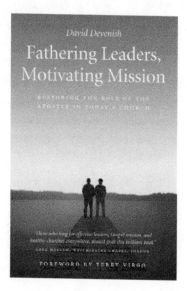

Fathering Leaders, Motivating Mission

Restoring the Role of the Apostle in Today's Church

David Devenish

978-1-86024-837-5

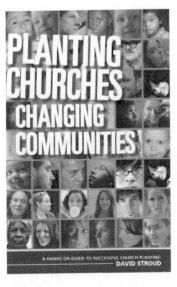

Planting Churches, Changing Communities

A Hands-On Guide to Successful Church Planting

David Stroud

978-1-86024-856-0

What On Earth is the Church For?

A Blueprint for the Future for Church-Based Mission and Social Action

David Devenish

978-1-86024-537-4